BMA's
REASONING
Trainer Plus

Class 6

BRAIN MAPPING
A C A D E M Y
Mapping Your Future

www.bmatalent.com

Published by:

Brain Mapping Academy
#16–11–16/1/B, First Floor, Farhath Hospital Road,
Saleem Nagar, Malakpet, Hyderabad–500 036.
✆ : 040–66135169, 65165169
E-mail: info@bmatalent.com
Website: www.bmatalent.com

Publication Team

Chief Mentor   :   Srinivas Kalluri

Authors   :   Y.S. Srinivasu

Design and Typing :   Muhammed Irfan Khan

Cover Design   :   D. Nagendra Raju

ISBN : 978-93-82058-05-2

Disclaimer

Every care has been taken by the compilers and publishers to give correct, complete and updated information. In case there is any omission, printing mistake or any other error which might have crept in inadvertently, neither the compiler / publisher nor any of the distributors take any legal responsibility.

In case of any dispute, all matters are subjected to the exclusive jurisdiction of the courts in Hyderabad only.

First Edition : 2012

Printed at:
Sri Vinayaka Art Printers, Hyderabad.

Preface

The process of learning is dependent on one's ability to think logically and reason quickly and effectively. These two factors are hence very crucial to a child's progress in education.

Though some children might show this ability naturally, logical analysis and effective reasoning are skills that can be developed and honed. This book has been specifically designed by experts to cater to this need of students of all classes - for the development of their reasoning and logic skills.

Reasoning and logic skills are an integral part of a wide range of subjects such as Math, Science, Design and Technology, etc. These skills are also vital in our day to day lives.

The questions in this book are styled for standardized tests. The questions on problem solving, critical thinking, judgment and decision making skills equip students to prepare and face any competitive exam where reasoning is an important part.

This book trains the learner's mind to:

- Look at problems with different perspectives through observation, exploration and critical thinking.
- Integrate the application of Math to problem solving.
- Think critically, reason logically and express mathematically.
- Practice, investigate, evaluate and learn with understanding.
- Develop positive attitude towards Mathematics.

With regular practice in solving these questions, the student will feel more confident and better equipped to tackle challenging problems not only in Mathematics examinations but also in real-life situations.

This book is a part of the curriculum designed for Reasoning for classes 1 to 10. It provides a graded pattern of questions with increasing levels of difficulty. It is advised to introduce this book as a part of the curriculum.

The catalyst to boost and sharpen
Logical thinking and reasoning skills.

Design Framework

All the topics in this book are grouped as under :

VERBAL REASONING

NON-VERBAL REASONING

For each question type, a worked out example shows exactly what the question demands, and explains how to tackle it in three or four clear steps. The approach is systematic and highly effective, lending itself to active learning.

- Each topic is dealt with in a separate unit.

- Each unit begins with a brief explanation of the question types and the procedure to solve them.

- Sufficient Number of examples with clear step-by-step explanation to arrive at the solution

- Ample number of practice questions.

This book contains several interesting and investigative problems with worked out examples and explanations.

CONTENTS

List of useful symbols

VERBAL REASONING

1. Hidden works .... 11 to 13

2. Jumbled words .... 14 to 15

3. Odd one out .... 16 to 18

4. Matching Pairs .... 19 to 21

5. Series .... 22 to 26

6. Using letters for numbers .... 27 to 28

7. Puzzle test .... 29 to 32

8. Analytical reasoning .... 33 to 41

9. Mathematical reasoning .... 42 to 52

10. Break the codes .... 53 to 63

NON-VERBAL REASONING

Spatial sense .... 64 to 69

11. Which one is different ? .... 70 to 80

12. Analogy .... 81 to 97

13. What comes next ? .... 98 to 110

14. Mirror images .... 111 to 123

15. Paper folding .... 124 to 138

16. Opened out .... 139 to 147

Key .... 148 to 151

LIST OF USEFUL SYMBOLS

Reasoning questions combine three elements
SHAPES, FILLS & LINES.

SHAPES

These comprise all 'closed' geometrical shapes.

(i) Triangles

Equilateral   Scalene   Isosceles

(ii) Quadrilaterals

Square   Rectangle   Trapezium   Isosceles Trapezium

Kite   Parallelogram   Rhombus   Arrowhead

(iii) Regular Polygons

Pentagon   Hexagon   Heptagon   Octagon

(iv) Circular Shapes

Circle   Semicircle   Ellipse   Quadrant

(v) Irregular Polygons
Irregular shapes have unequal sides and angles

General
Quadrilateral

Pentagon

Hexagon

(i) Straight - edged shapes

Straight Arrows   Sea Horse   Pencil

Boot

4 - pointed   5 - pointed   6 - pointed   Speaker   Cross
Stars

Envelope   House   Letters   Boat   Bow Tie

(ii) Curved Shapes

Shields   Curved Arrows   Flower

Bean   Moon   Heart   Letters   Wizard's   Bone
Hat

Bulb   Ribbon   Wheel   Loaf   Matchstick   Phone
or Flag

© Brain Mapping Academy

FILLS

'Closed' shape fills comprise four different categories:

(i) Block Fills

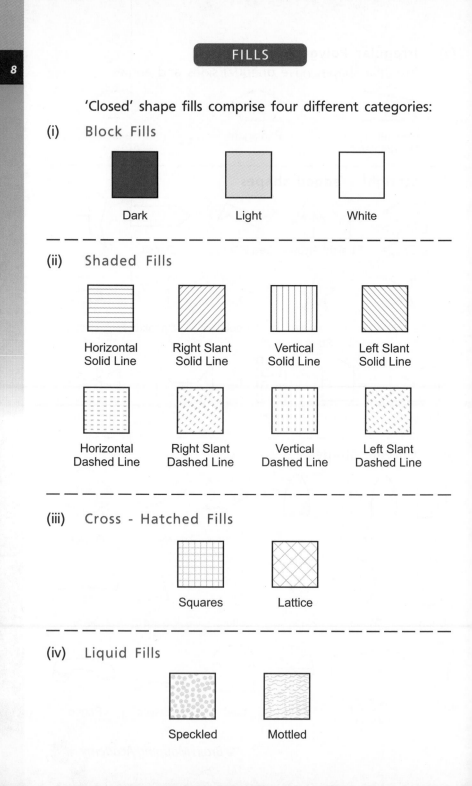

| Dark | Light | White |

(ii) Shaded Fills

| Horizontal Solid Line | Right Slant Solid Line | Vertical Solid Line | Left Slant Solid Line |

| Horizontal Dashed Line | Right Slant Dashed Line | Vertical Dashed Line | Left Slant Dashed Line |

(iii) Cross - Hatched Fills

| Squares | Lattice |

(iv) Liquid Fills

| Speckled | Mottled |

LINES

All line types have three main properties:

1. Solid   Dashed   Dotted

2. Straight   Curved

3. Thin   Thick

LINE SHAPES

These comprise everyday recognisable 'Open' shapes.

(i) Straight - edged Shapes

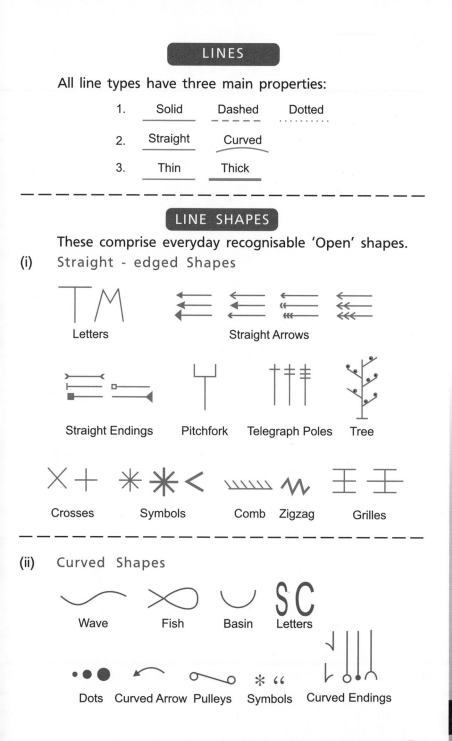

Letters

Straight Arrows

Straight Endings   Pitchfork   Telegraph Poles   Tree

Crosses   Symbols   Comb   Zigzag   Grilles

(ii) Curved Shapes

Wave   Fish   Basin   Letters

Dots   Curved Arrow   Pulleys   Symbols   Curved Endings

© Brain Mapping Academy

In these type of questions you are given a sentence in which a four letter word is hidden between two words. The letters at the end of one word and the letters at the beginning of the next word make up a new four letter word. You are required to locate the pair of words that contain the hidden word.

As the hidden word is always a four letter word, it could be the last three letters and first letter of a pair of words, the last two and first two or the last one and first three. A good strategy is to look at the whole sentence and see if the answer jumps out at you. If not, go through each pair of words systematically - look at last three letters of each word and the first letter of the next word and then move along one letter at a time. Do this with each pair of words until you find the answer. Some children find it easier to position their fingers or thumbs over the words so that they can only see four letters at a time.

Example 1

Identify the pair of words that contain the hidden word.

$$\text{We must welcome the new boy.}$$
$$\;\; 1 \quad\; 2 \qquad 3 \qquad\;\, 4 \;\;\, 5 \quad\; 6$$

(A) 2, 3   (B) 4, 5   (C) 5, 6   (D) 1, 2

Answer: (B)

Explanation:

The answer is T H E N because it is hidden between the two words 'the new'.

All 3 letters of 'the' and the first letter of 'new' form the hidden word, as shown by the underlining.

(The answer is not, 'come', as this is hidden in one word, instead of between TWO words)

TRY THESE

Directions: 1 to 12:

In the questions below you are given a sentence in which a four letter word is hidden between two words. Locate the pair of the words that contain the hidden word.

1.
$$\overset{1}{\text{Re}}\,\overset{2}{\text{asoning}}\,\overset{3}{\text{books}}\,\overset{4}{\text{are}}\,\overset{5}{\text{still}}\,\overset{6}{\text{great}}\,\text{fun.}$$

(A) 3, 2   (B) 6, 1   (C) 3, 4   (D) 1, 4

2.
$$\overset{1}{\text{For}}\,\overset{2}{\text{my}}\,\overset{3}{\text{birthday}}\,\overset{4}{\text{I}}\,\overset{5}{\text{want}}\,\overset{6}{\text{more}}\,\overset{7}{\text{sweets.}}$$

(A) 3, 1   (B) 7, 4   (C) 5, 6   (D) 1, 2

3.
$$\overset{1}{\text{It}}\,\overset{2}{\text{is}}\,\overset{3}{\text{well}}\,\overset{4}{\text{hidden}}\,\overset{5}{\text{there.}}$$

(A) 6, 1   (B) 4, 5   (C) 1, 2   (D) 3, 5

4.
$$\overset{1}{\text{If}}\,\overset{2}{\text{you}}\,\overset{3}{\text{are}}\,\overset{4}{\text{clever}}\,\overset{5}{\text{you}}\,\overset{6}{\text{can}}\,\overset{7}{\text{make}}\,\overset{8}{\text{a}}\,\overset{9}{\text{word.}}$$

(A) 2, 4   (B) 8, 6   (C) 4, 5   (D) 3, 1

5.
$$\overset{1}{\text{The}}\,\overset{2}{\text{robe}}\,\overset{3}{\text{stuck}}\,\overset{4}{\text{out}}\,\overset{5}{\text{because}}\,\overset{6}{\text{it}}\,\overset{7}{\text{was}}\,\overset{8}{\text{green.}}$$

(A) 5, 6   (B) 7, 8   (C) 2, 3   (D) 4, 5

6.
$$\overset{1}{\text{Although}}\,\overset{2}{\text{Harry}}\,\overset{3}{\text{was}}\,\overset{4}{\text{petrified,}}\,\overset{5}{\text{he}}\,\overset{6}{\text{raised}}\,\overset{7}{\text{his}}\,\overset{8}{\text{wand.}}$$

(A) 2, 3   (B) 6, 7   (C) 4, 5   (D) 7, 8

7.
$$\overset{1}{\text{Moses}}\,\overset{2}{\text{often}}\,\overset{3}{\text{wondered}}\,\overset{4}{\text{if}}\,\overset{5}{\text{he}}\,\overset{6}{\text{had}}\,\overset{7}{\text{made}}\,\overset{8}{\text{the}}\,\overset{9}{\text{right}}\,\overset{10}{\text{decision.}}$$

(A) 4, 5   (B) 1, 2   (C) 7, 8   (D) 9, 10

8.
$$\overset{1}{\text{David}}\,\overset{2}{\text{owned}}\,\overset{3}{\text{half}}\,\overset{4}{\text{the}}\,\overset{5}{\text{shares}}\,\overset{6}{\text{in}}\,\overset{7}{\text{Reliance}}$$

(A) 3, 4   (B) 6, 7   (C) 1, 2   (D) 5, 6

9. $\overset{1}{\text{The}}$ $\overset{2}{\text{church}}$ $\overset{3}{\text{in}}$ $\overset{4}{\text{this}}$ $\overset{5}{\text{lane}}$ $\overset{6}{\text{was}}$ $\overset{7}{\text{lit}}$ $\overset{8}{\text{by}}$ $\overset{9}{\text{a}}$ $\overset{10}{\text{bright}}$ $\overset{11}{\text{light.}}$

(A) 2, 3　　　(B) 5, 6　　　(C) 3, 4　　　(D) 8, 9

10. $\overset{1}{\text{Puneete}}$ $\overset{2}{\text{argued}}$ $\overset{3}{\text{his}}$ $\overset{4}{\text{case}}$ $\overset{5}{\text{in}}$ $\overset{6}{\text{court}}$ $\overset{7}{\text{before}}$ $\overset{8}{\text{the}}$ $\overset{9}{\text{judge.}}$

(A) 3, 4　　　(B) 7, 8　　　(C) 1, 2　　　(D) 5, 6

11. $\overset{1}{\text{The}}$ $\overset{2}{\text{class}}$ $\overset{3}{\text{of}}$ $\overset{4}{\text{yoga}}$ $\overset{5}{\text{included}}$ $\overset{6}{\text{a}}$ $\overset{7}{\text{free}}$ $\overset{8}{\text{mat.}}$

(A) 6, 7　　　(B) 7, 8　　　(C) 4, 5　　　(D) 2, 3

12. $\overset{1}{\text{The}}$ $\overset{2}{\text{dutiful}}$ $\overset{3}{\text{librarian}}$ $\overset{4}{\text{searched}}$ $\overset{5}{\text{for}}$ $\overset{6}{\text{a}}$ $\overset{7}{\text{book.}}$

(A) 3, 4　　　(B) 2, 3　　　(C) 5, 6　　　(D) 6, 7

2 Chapter — JUMBLED WORDS

Example 1

The letters of a word for the clue is given to help you find the words that have been jumbled up in the options. Identify the one that matches the clue.

1. A number

   (A) YFDRIA   (B) OERS   (C) VESEN   (D) NORI

Answer: (C)

Explanation:

Option (A) → Friday, Option (B) → Ores, Option (C) → Seven, Option (D) → Iron

Hence, option (C) is the correct answer.

2. Contains stories

   (A) KBOO   (B) AET   (C) CUIJE   (D) RUPEOE

Answer: (A)

Explanation:

Option (A) → Book, Option (B) → Tea, eat, ate? Option (C) → Juice, Option (D) → Europe

Hence, option (A) is the correct answer.

TRY THESE

Directions from 1 to 11:

In the following questions the letters of the words have been jumbled up. Find the word each time with the help of clues given.

1. A kind of vegetable

   (A) OTRNH   (B) PRECOP   (C) OPTTAO   (D) NZCI

2. Hospital worker

   (A) ABKLC   (B) TCRODO   (C) KTUCEB   (D) LKMI

3. View computer
    (A) ARMCOR (B) RMINOTO (C) ARNI (D) ICHN

4. Air transport
    (A) LAPEN (B) OTRNH (C) GWNUA (D) ADSUNY

5. A kind of fruit
    (A) DRYA (B) ECNBH (C) GMOAN (D) SUTOH

6. Residence
    (A) OSEHU (B) EUJN (C) TOFO (D) RIVELS

7. Sharp cutting edge
    (A) VTIEOL (B) LEDAB (C) ENCIDSTA (D) SIAA

8. Leap over
    (A) GITLGHN (B) MRIAECA (C) UPJM (D) LKMI

9. Something to sit on
    (A) EUMRSM (B) ATLBE (C) CTAPRE (D) FOAS

10. A measure of time
    (A) HRCIA (B) ROHU (C) ABKLC (D) KITCCRE

11. Double or 2 times
    (A) ENICDSTA (B) PRAIL (C) CWIET (D) LLOOBFTA

3 Chapter

Example 1

Find the odd one among the following.

(A) 11   (B) 13   (C) 15   (D) 17

Answer: (C)

Explanation:

All except 15 are prime numbers

Example 2

Find the odd one among the following.

(A) ABC   (B) BCD   (C) CDE   (D) DEF

Answer: (D)

Explanation:

In except BCD, there is a vowel and two consonants but in BCD all the three are consonants.

TRY THESE

1. Find the odd one out.

   (A) U   (B) O   (C) P   (D) I

2. Which one is different from the others?

   (A) AB   (B) DF   (C) GH   (D) JK

3. Identify the one that does not belong to the group.

   (A) ZYX   (B) WUV   (C) TSR   (D) QPO

REASONING TRAINER Plus

4. Identify the one which is different from the others.

   (A) BD   (B) CI   (C) DP   (D) EV

5. Find the odd one out.

   (A) MN   (B) IR   (C) SF   (D) OL

6. Which one is different from the others.

   (A) BD   (B) FL   (C) JS   (D) KV

7. Identify the one that does not belong to the group.

   (A) LMN   (B) LKJ   (C) UTS   (D) FED

8. Identify the one which is different from the others.

   (A) AA   (B) BB   (C) EEEEE   (D) DDDD

9. Find the odd one out.

   (A) 1234   (B) 6789   (C) 3456   (D) 2354

10. Which one is different from the others.

    (A) 324   (B) 243   (C) 432   (D) 234

11. Identify the one that does not belong to the group.

    (A) 121   (B) 169   (C) 225   (D) 289

12. Identify the one which is different from the others.

    (A) 24   (B) 32   (C) 48   (D) 72

13. Find the odd one out.

    (A) 46   (B) 35   (C) 91   (D) 56

14. Which one is different from the others.

    (A) 27   (B) 125   (C) 8   (D) 64

15. Identify the one that does not belong to the group.

    (A) 927   (B) 816   (C) 725   (D) 624

16. Identify the one which is different from the others.

    (A) 1002   (B) 2003   (C) 3004   (D) 4005

17. Find the odd one out.

    (A) 11B   (B) 22D   (C) 33G   (D) 44H

18. Which one is different from the others.

   (A) PQ9   (B) QR8   (C) SR7   (D) ST6

19. Identify the one that does not belong to the group.

   (A) AZ11   (B) BY22   (C) CX32   (D) DW44

20. Identify the one which is different from the others.

   (A) 123D   (B) 234F   (C) 456G   (D) 567I

21. Find the odd one out.

   (A) YFDRIA   (B) URATSYAD
   (C) MDOANY   (D) PRAIL

22. Which one is different from the others.

   (A) NREGE   (B) LBUE
   (C) ORCLUO   (D) VTIEOL

23. Identify the one that does not belong to the group.

   (A) ECNBH   (B) SLOTO
   (C) HRCIA   (D) CARPET

24. Identify the one which is different from the others.

   (A) REMVONBE   (B) CEDBERME
   (C) EUJN   (D) ERBMETPES

Example 1

Find the matching pair.

AZBY isto CXDW as EVFU isto [?]

(A) GTHS   (B) GHTS   (C) GSTH   (D) TGSH

Answer: (A)

Explanation:

As   A $\xrightarrow{+2}$ C   similarly,   E $\xrightarrow{+2}$ G

Z $\xrightarrow{-2}$ X   V $\xrightarrow{-2}$ T

B $\xrightarrow{+2}$ D   F $\xrightarrow{+2}$ H

Y $\xrightarrow{-2}$ W   U $\xrightarrow{-2}$ S

Example 2

Find the matching pair.

ABC isto ZYX as CBA isto [?]

(A) XYZ   (B) BCA   (C) YZX   (D) ZXY

Answer: (A)

Explanation:

CBA is the reverse of ABC. Similarly XYZ is the reverse of ZYX.

Example 3

Find the matching pair.

MXN isto 13 x 14 as FXR isto (?)

(A) 14 × 15   (B) 5 × 17   (C) 6 × 18   (D) 7 × 19

Answer: (C)

Explanation:

The positions of M and N in the order of alphabets are 13 and 14 respectively.

Similarly, the positions of F and R are 6 and 18 respectively.

TRY THESE

1. Find the matching pair.

    12 isto 24 as 21 isto (?)

    (A) 25   (B) 32   (C) 35   (D) 42

2. Find the matching pair.

    2 isto 8 as 5 isto (?)

    (A) 25   (B) 125   (C) 50   (D) 250

3. Find the matching pair.

    322120 isto 321920 as 324342 isto (?)

    (A) 324142   (B) 324132   (C) 323143   (D) 323319

4. Find the matching pair.

    13 isto 19 as (?) isto 31

    (A) 21   (B) 23   (C) 25   (D) 26

5. Find the matching pair.

    TSR isto FED as WVU isto (?)

    (A) CAB   (B) MLK   (C) PQS   (D) GFH

6. Find the matching pair.

    CAT isto DDY as BIG isto (?)

    (A) CLL   (B) CLM   (C) CML   (D) CEP

7. Find the matching pair.

    AG isto IO as EK isto (?)

    (A) LR   (B) MS   (C) PV   (D) SY

8. Find the matching pair.

    ACEG isto DFHJ as QSUW isto (?)

    (A) KMNP   (B) MNPR   (C) TQST   (D) TVXZ

9. Find the matching pair.

    EGIK isto FILO as FHJL isto (?)

    (A) GJMP   (B) GMJP   (C) JGMP   (D) JGPM

10. Find the matching pair.

    ACE isto FHJ as OQS isto (?)

    (A) PRT   (B) RTU   (C) TVX   (D) UWY

5 Chapter

SERIES

Example 1

Find the next number in the series below.

$$(3) \quad (9) \quad (10) \quad (30) \quad (31) \quad (?)$$

(A) 38   (B) 46   (C) 78   (D) 93

Answer: (D)

Explanation:

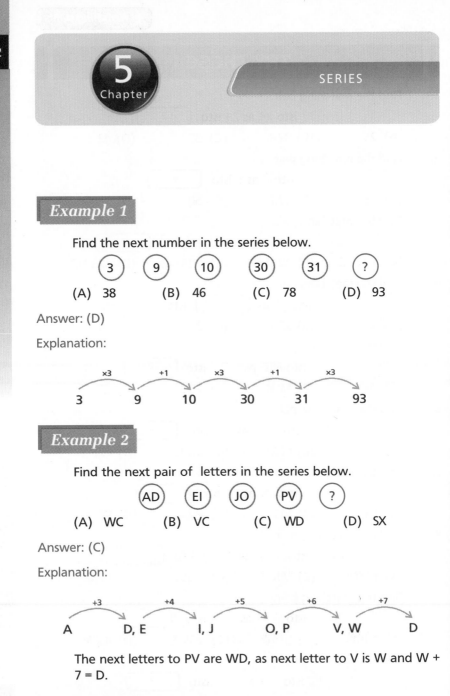

Example 2

Find the next pair of letters in the series below.

$$(AD) \quad (EI) \quad (JO) \quad (PV) \quad (?)$$

(A) WC   (B) VC   (C) WD   (D) SX

Answer: (C)

Explanation:

The next letters to PV are WD, as next letter to V is W and W + 7 = D.

Example 3

Find the missing number in the following series.

(A) 52   (B) 54   (C) 44   (D) 42

Answer: (D)

Explanation:

2   6   14   26   42   62

+4   +8   +12   +16   +20

The difference of each successive number is increased by 4. Hence, number 42 will fill up the blank space.

Example 4

Find the missing number in the following series.

① 1   ⑧ 8   ㉗ 27   ㉔ 64   ? ?   ㉒ 216

(A) 127   (B) 125   (C) 124   (D) 128

Answer: (B)

Explanation:

1   8   27   64 $\boxed{125}$ 216

↓   ↓   ↓   ↓   ↓   ↓

1^3 2^3 3^3 4^3 5^3 6^3

TRY THESE

Complete each of the following series by choosing the right answer from the options given.

1. (B) (E) (H) (K) (N) (?)

   (A) P   (B) Q   (C) R   (D) S

2. (C) (D) (F) (I) (M) (?)

   (A) P   (B) Q   (C) R   (D) S

3. (Y) (W) (U) (S) (Q) (?)

   (A) O   (B) P   (C) Q   (D) R

4. (A) (Z) (B) (Y) (C) (?)

   (A) D   (B) W   (C) X   (D) E

5. (AB) (cd) (EF) (gh) (?)

   (A) Hi   (B) hi   (C) ij   (D) IJ

6. (W) (A) (E) (I) (M) (?)

   (A) Q   (B) P   (C) R   (D) O

7. (M) (W) (L) (X) (K) (Y) (?)

   (A) I   (B) J   (C) K   (D) M

8. (YB) (XD) (WF) (VH) (?)

   (A) UV   (B) IL   (C) TN   (D) UJ

9. (AJ) (DK) (GL) (JM) (?)

   (A) CF   (B) IW   (C) MN   (D) JO

10. (BI) (EK) (HM) (KO) (?)

   (A) PO   (B) NQ   (C) ZX   (D) GH

11. (XO) (WL) (VI) (UF) (?)

   (A) IN   (B) FO   (C) TI   (D) TC

12. (NW) (KT) (HQ) (EN) (?)

   (A) BK   (B) SL   (C) IB   (D) TX

REASONING TRAINER Plus

13. Z S W O T K Q G ? ?

(A) N, C   (B) N, D   (C) O, C   (D) O, D

14. CG FH II LJ OK ?

(A) PM   (B) QL
(C) PL   (D) RL

15. 81 64 49 36 25 ?

(A) 16   (B) 17   (C) 24   (D) 35

16. 49 58 67 76 85 ?

(A) 91   (B) 92   (C) 94   (D) 95

17. 1 2 6 24 120 ?

(A) 540   (B) 680   (C) 700   (D) 720

18. 800 400 200 100 50 ?

(A) 20   (B) 25   (C) 30   (D) 35

19. 49 37 27 19 13 ?

(A) 5   (B) 7   (C) 9   (D) 11

20. 2 10 20 32 46 ?

(A) 62   (B) 64   (C) 78   (D) 80

21. 1 8 27 64 125 ?

(A) 150   (B) 216   (C) 228   (D) 236

22. 2 5 9 14 20 ?

(A) 24   (B) 25   (C) 26   (D) 27

23. 4 6 10 18 34 ?

(A) 60   (B) 66   (C) 72   (D) 80

24. 90 76 63 51 40 ?

(A) 20   (B) 25   (C) 30   (D) 32

25. 2 3 5 7 11 13 ?

(A) 15   (B) 16   (C) 17   (D) 18

26. (31) (29) (32) (30) (33) (?)

    (A) 30   (B) 31   (C) 32   (D) 33

27. (1) (10) (100) (1000) (?)

    (A) 1000   (B) 10,000   (C) 1,00,000 (D) 1,10,000

28. (729) (243) (81) (27) (9) (?)

    (A) 3   (B) 5   (C) 7   (D) 9

Directions from 29 to 34:

The following questions show three sets of numbers on each line, related in the same way. Mark the missing number.

29. (3) (9) (3)   (4) (28) (7)   (9) (?) (6)

    (A) 3   (B) 15   (C) 54   (D) 72

30. (27) (3) (9)   (36) (6) (6)   (32) (?) (4)

    (A) 4   (B) 6   (C) 8   (D) 10

31. (25) (32) (9)   (7) (11) (6)   (10) (?) (9)

    (A) 16   (B) 17   (C) 18   (D) 20

32. (7) (50) (7)   (4) (13) (3)   (8) (?) (6)

    (A) 45   (B) 46   (C) 47   (D) 49

33. (39) (25) (14)   (81) (74) (7)   (55) (?) (19)

    (A) 32   (B) 34   (C) 36   (D) 74

34. (4) (20) (12)   (5) (23) (14)   (7) (?) (16)

    (A) 27   (B) 23   (C) 35   (D) 29

6 Chapter

Example 1

1. If P = 7, Q = 2, R = 4, and S = 1 then Q + R + S =

   (A) Q   (B) R   (C) P   (D) S

Answer: (C)

Explanation:

$$2 + 4 + 1 = 7$$
$$Q + R + S = (\underline{P})$$

TRY THESE

Directions from 1 to 15:

In the following questions letters take the place of numbers. Complete each of the sums and identify the letter that gives the answer.

1. If P = 5, Q = 4, R = 1, S = 2, and T = 0,
   then Q + R − P = ?

   (A) Q   (B) R   (C) S   (D) T

2. If P = 4, Q = 6, R = 10, S = 20, and T = 22,
   then P × Q − P = ?

   (A) P   (B) S   (C) T   (D) Q

3. If P = 2, Q = 3, R = 5, S = 7, and T = 12,
   then R + S = ?

   (A) T   (B) Q   (C) P   (D) R

4. If P = 9, Q = 81, R = 27, S = 3, and T = 18,
   then Q ÷ R = ?

   (A) R   (B) T   (C) S   (D) P

5. If P = 9, Q = 81, R = 27, S = 3, and T = 18,
   then R ÷ S × P = ?

   (A) S   (B) Q   (C) T   (D) R

27

6. If P = 18, Q = 10, R = 14, S = 16, and T = 20, then what is S – R + P = ?

(A) P   (B) Q   (C) S   (D) T

7. If P = 2, Q = 4, R = 11, S = 21, and T = 25, then, what is $(R \times R - S) \div T$ = ?

(A) R   (B) Q   (C) P   (D) S

8. If P = 2, Q = 4, R = 5, S = 20, and T = 100, then, what is $T \div Q - R$ = ?

(A) P   (B) Q   (C) S   (D) R

9. If P = 4, Q = 7, R = 9, S = 12, and T = 20, then, what is $S \div P \times R - Q$ = ?

(A) T   (B) P   (C) Q   (D) R

10. If P = 13, Q = 25, R = 30, S = 50, and T = 73, then, what is T – P – R?

(A) T   (B) S   (C) R   (D) Q

11. If P = 0, Q = 1, R = 22, S = 35, and T = 57, then, what is $R + S \times P$ = ?

(A) R   (B) P   (C) Q   (D) S

12. If P = 1, Q = 3, R = 5, and S = 9 then P + Q + R = ?

(A) Q   (B) P   (C) S   (D) R

13. If P = 9, Q = 6, R = 15, and S = 3 then R – P – S = ?

(A) S   (B) P   (C) R   (D) Q

14. If P = 20, Q = 16, R = 6, and S = 2 then P – R + S = ?

(A) R   (B) S   (C) Q   (D) P

15. If P = 5, Q = 4, R = 9, and S = 11 then $P \times Q - S$ = ?

(A) P   (B) Q   (C) R   (D) S

Example 1

The information below is about 4 children, John, Katrina, Leena and Madan and the flavours of fruit juices they like.

(i) John and Katrina are the only two who like both apple and orange.

(ii) Katrina and Madan are the only two who like both orange and banana.

(iii) Leena and John are the only two who like both grapefruit and strawberry.

P. Who likes orange, but not banana juice?

(A) Katrina   (B) John   (C) Leena   (D) Madan

Q. Who likes orange, banana and apple?

(A) Leena   (B) Madan   (C) Katrina   (D) John

Answer: P – (B), Q – (C)

Explanation:

A grid has been drawn to show the information using the initials of the 4 children. The box has been ticked for each flavour that the child likes. The box is left empty ☐ for each flavour that the child does not like.

	J	K	L	M
Apple	✓	✓		
Orange	✓	✓		✓
Banana		✓		✓
Grapefruit	✓		✓	
Strawberry	✓		✓	

P The answer is John because, in the grid only John has both the 'orange box' ticked and the banana box empty.

Q The answer is Katrina because, in the grid only Katrina` has these three flavours ticked.

© Brain Mapping Academy

TRY THESE

Directions from 1 to 5:

Ali, Bacchan, Chote, Divya and Helen are five children at the same school.

i) Bacchan and Ali like English, but the others do not.

ii) Ali and Chote are the only ones who do not like Maths.

iii) All like Science, except Bacchan and Helen.

1. Who likes English but not Maths?

   (A) Divya   (B) Ali   (C) Bacchan   (D) Chote

2. Who does not like English and also does not like Science?
   (A) Ali   (B) Divya   (C) Chote   (D) Helen

3. Who likes English, but not Science?

   (A) Ali   (B) Bacchan   (C) Helen   (D) Divya

4. How many children who like English also like Maths?

   (A) 4   (B) 6   (C) 1   (D) 2

5. Which child who likes Science also likes Maths?

   (A) Divya   (B) Helen   (C) Bacchan   (D) Ali

Direction from 6 to 10:

There are five friends, Sushma, Rajiv, Bijay, Asha and Nisha.
Rajiv and Asha like football, but the others like tennis.
Only Nisha, Rajiv and Sushma like going abroad for their holidays.
All but Asha and Bijay have piano lessons.

6. Who likes football and also likes going abroad for their holidays?

   (A) Bijay   (B) Sushma   (C) Rajiv   (D) Nisha

7. Who likes football but does not have piano lessons?
   (A) Asha   (B) Nisha   (C) Bijay   (D) Sushma

8. Who likes tennis but does not have piano lessons?

   (A) Nisha   (B) Sushma   (C) Asha   (D) Bijay

9. How many children who like tennis also have piano lessons?
   (A) Four   (B) Two   (C) One   (D) Three

10. How many children who like going abroad do not have piano lessons?

(A) 3   (B) 5   (C) 0   (D) 8

Directions from 11 to 15:

Study the following information carefully and answer the given questions:

i) Q and T are good in Arts and Games.

ii) P and Q are good in Games and Science.

iii) P, S and R are good in Games and Social.

iv) R and P are good in Science and Mathematics.

v) S and T are good in History and Arts.

11. Who is good in Science, Social and Arts ?

(A) P   (B) Q   (C) S   (D) T

12. Who is good in Science, Social and Mathematics, but not in Games?

(A) P   (B) R   (C) Q   (D) S

13. Who is good in Games, Social and Arts ?

(A) P   (B) Q   (C) R   (D) T

14. Who is good in Social, Science, Games and Mathematics ?

(A) P   (B) Q   (C) R   (D) S

15. Who is good in Science, Arts and Games ?

(A) P   (B) Q   (C) S   (D) T

Directions from 16 to 18:

Ravi and Kunal are good in Hockey and Volleyball. Sachin and Ravi are good in Hockey and Baseball. Gaurav and Kunal are good in Cricket and Volleyball. Sachin, Gaurav and Michael are good in Football and Baseball.

16. Who is good in Hockey, Cricket and Volleyball ?

(A) Sachin   (B) Kunal   (C) Ravi   (D) Gaurav

17. Who is good in Baseball, Cricket, Volleyball and Football ?

(A) Sachin   (B) Kunal   (C) Gaurav   (D) Ravi

18. Who is good in Baseball, Volleyball and Hockey?

(A) Sachin   (B) Kunal   (C) Ravi   (D) Gaurav

31

© Brain Mapping Academy

Directions from 19 to 20:

Study the following information and answer the questions given below it:

i) Saketh, Kartik and Kabeer are intelligent.

ii) Saketh, Rajesh and Rakesh are hard-working.

iii) Rajesh, Kabeer and Rakesh are honest.

iv) Saketh, Kartik and Rakesh are ambitious.

19. Which of the following persons is neither hard-working nor ambitious ?

(A) Saketh   (B) Kartik   (C) Kabeer   (D) Rajesh

20. Which of the following persons is neither honest nor hard-working but is ambitious ?

(A) Saketh   (B) Kartik   (D) Rajesh   (D) Kabeer

Objective ///

- To make the student practise experiencing peace in pandimonium.

Questions of sitting arrangement are based on a set of information containing certain conditions. Candidates are required to arrange the objects either in a row or in a circle on the basis of given conditions. Information given in the question is presented in distorted form to create confusion and to test candidate's ability to analyse the information step by step in order to answer the question correctly.

Following examples will help students understand the pattern of such questions and also methods to solve them.

Example 1

Directions: In a class there are seven students (including boys and girls) A, B, C, D, E, F and G. They sit on three benches I, II and III such that there are at least two students on each bench and at least one girl on each bench. C who is a girl student, does not sit with A, E and D. F the boy student sits with only B. A sits on the bench I with his best friends. G sits on the bench III. E is the brother of C?

a. How many girls are there. Out of these 7 students?

(A) 3   (B) 4

(C) 3 or 4   (D) Data inadequate

Answer: (C)

Explanation:

Using the conditions given we can infer that A and D can be either girl or a boy. One of them will sit with E.

Table 1

Bench I	A	E	D
Bench II	F	B	
Bench III	G	C	
☐ Boy	○ Girl		

The number of girls is either 3 or 4.

b. Who sits with C?

    (A) B   (B) D   (C) G   (D)E

Answer: (C)

Explanation:

Refer Table 1.

c. Which of the following is the group of girls?

    (A) BAC   (B) BCD   (C) BFC   (D) CDF

Answer: (B)

Explanation:

Refer Table 1.

d. On which bench there are three students?

    (A) I   (B) II   (C) III   (D) I or II

Answer: (A)

Explanation:

Refer Table 1.

Example 2

Which letter is 8th to the left of the 13th letter from the left of the English alphabet?

(A) F   (B) H   (C) G   (D) E

Answer: (D)

Explanation:

13 - 8 = 5 (From left to left) 5th letter from the left is E.

As E is given at option D. Hence (D) is the correct answer.

Example 3

Which letter is 10th to the right of the 15th letter to the right of the English alphabet?

(A) S   (B) T   (C) V   (D) U

Answer: (C)

Explanation:

15 - 10 = 5 (From right to right)

Now 5th from the right is required.

27 - 5 = 22

Hence 22nd from the left is V. Which is in (C).

Example 4

If all the letters of the English alphabet are written in reverse order, then which letter will be 6th to the left of the third letter from the right?

(A) H   (B) N   (C) S   (D) I

Answer: (D)

Explanation:

Letters in reverse order:

Z Y X W V U T S R Q P O N M L K J I H G F E D C B A.

Then 3 + 6 = 9 (Right to left).

Now 9th from the left in original is I which is given in (D).

Example 5

If second half of the English alphabet is written in reverse order, then which will be the 8th letter to the right of the 7th letter from the left?

(A) Y   (B) X   (C) W   (D) V

Answer: (A)

Explanation:

On writing the second half of the English alphabet in reverse order:

A B C D E F G H I J K L M Z Y X W V U T S R Q P O N

Now 7 + 8 = 15 (Left to right)

Now 15th letter from the left is Y.

Example 6

Which letter will be 8th to the right of the 9th letter from the left end of the English alphabet?

(A) R   (B) Q   (C) P   (D) S

Answer: (B)

Explanation:

9 + 8 = 17 (From left to right).

Now 17th letter from left is 'Q' which is in (B).

Example 7

Which letter will be 9th to the left of the 7th letter from the right?

(A) L   (B) K   (C) N   (D) H

Answer: (B)

Explanation:

> 9 + 7 = 16 (From right to left).
>
> Then 27 - 16 = 11.
>
> Hence 11th letter from the left is K which is in (B).

Example 8

If first half of the English alphabet is written in reverse order, then which letter will be 9th to the left of the 18th letter from the left?

(A) H   (B) E   (C) G   (D) L

Answer: (B)

Explanation:

> On writing the first half of the English alphabet in reverse order:
>
> M L K J I H G F E D C B A N O P Q R S T U V W X Y Z
>
> Now 18 - 9 = 9 (Left to left)
>
> 9th letter from the left is E.

Example 9

In the English alphabet which letter is exactly midway between the 5th letter from the left and 7th letter from the right?

(A) K   (B) L   (C) M   (D) J

Answer: (B)

Explanation:

> A B C D E F G H I J K L M N O P Q R S T U V W X Y Z.
>
> Fifth letter from the left is E and 7th letter from the right is S.
>
> Now L is just midway between E and S.

TRY THESE

1. If only the first half of the given alphabet is reversed, how many letters will be there between K and R?

(A) 6   (B) 10   (C) 14   (D) 16

2. If A interchanges position with B, similarly C and D interchange positions and so as E and F and so on upto Y and Z then which of the following will be seventh from the left?

(A) A   (B) F   (C) I   (D) H

3. If the order of the English alphabet is reversed, then which letter(s) would be exactly in the middle?

(A) L   (B) M   (C) N & M   (D) O

4. In the following series of letters, some definite order determines which of the next two letters in the correct order?

     A J K T U B I L S V C H M R W D G N Q X E F O ? ?

(A) P, Y   (B) P, Z   (C) Y, Z   (D) Z, A

5. Which letter will be the eighth to the right of the third letter of the second half of the English alphabet?

(A) V   (B) W   (C) X   (D) Y

6. Which letter is seventh to the right of the eighteenth letter from the right end of the alphabet?

(A) K   (B) O   (C) P   (D) R

7. Which letter is exactly midway between G and Q in alphabet?

(A) K   (B) L   (C) M   (D) N

Directions for 8 - 10: Read the following information carefully and answer the questions given below it:

i. There is a family of six members A, B, C, D, E and F.

ii. There are two married couples in the family and the family members represent three generations.

iii. Each member has a distinct choice of a colour amongst green, yellow, black, red, white and pink.

iv. No lady member likes either green or white.

v. C, who likes black color is the daughter-in-law of E.

vi. B is brother of F and son of D and likes pink.

8. Which of the following is the colour preference of A?

(A) Red   (B) Yellow
(C) Either Red or Yellow   (D) Cannot be determined

9. How many male members are there in the family?

(A) Two   (B) Three
(C) Four   (D) Cannot be determined

10. Which of the following is true about F?

(A) Brother of B   (B) Sister of B
(C) Daughter of C   (D) Either sister or brother of B

Directions for 11 - 15: Each of these questions is based on the information given below:

(i) A, B, C, D and E are five men sitting in a line facing to south - while M, N, O, P and Q, are five ladies sitting in a second line parallel to the first line and are facing to North.

(ii) B who is just next to the left of D, is opposite to Q.

(iii) C and N are diagonally opposite to each other.

(iv) E is opposite to-O who is just next right of M.

(v) P who is just to the left of Q, is opposite to D.

(vi) M is at one end of the line.

11. Who is sitting third to the right of O?

(A) Q   (B) N
(C) M   (D) Data inadequate

12. Which of the following pair is diagonally opposite to each other?

(A) E and Q   (B) B and O   (C) A and N   (D) A and M

13. If B shifts to the place of E, E shifts to the place of Q, and Q shifts to the place of B, then who will be the second to left of the person opposite to O?

(A) Q   (B) P   (C) E   (D) D

14. If O and P, A and E and B and Q interchange their positions, then who will be second person to the right of the person who is opposite to the person second of the right of P?

    (A) D   (B) A   (C) E   (D) O

15. In the original arrangement who is sitting just opposite to N?

    (A) B   (B) A   (C) C   (D) D

Directions for 16 - 18: P, Q, R, S, T, U, V and W are sitting round the circle and facing the centre:

  i.   P is second to the right T who is the neighbour of R and V.

 ii.   S is not the neighbour of P.

iii.   V is the neighbour of U.

iv.   Q is not between S and W. W is not between U and S.

16. What is the position of S?

    (A) Between U and V
    (B) Second to the right of P
    (C) To the immediate right of P
    (D) Data inadequate

17. Which two of the following are not neighbours?

    (A) R and V   (B) U and V   (C) R and P   (D) Q and W

18. Which of the following is correct?

    (A) P is to the immediate right of Q
    (B) R is between U and V
    (C) Q is to the immediate left of W
    (D) U is between W and S

19. Read the following instructions:

  i.   A, B and C are three boys while R, S and T are three girls. They are sitting such that the boys are facing the girls.

 ii.   A and R are diagonally opposite to each other.

iii.   C is not sitting at any of the ends.

iv.   T is left to R but opposite to C.

Find who is sitting opposite to B?

(A) R   (B) P   (C) Q   (D) S

Directions for 20 - 22: Read the instructions given below and answer the questions following them

i.   Eleven students A, B, C, D, E, F, G, H, I, J and K are sitting in the first line facing to the teacher.

ii.   D who is just to the left of F, is to the right of C at second place.

iii.   A is second to the right of E who is at one end.

iv.   J is the nearest neighbour of A and B and is to the left of G at third place.

v.   H is next to D to the right and is at the third place to the right of I.

20.   Find who is just in the middle.

(A) B   (B) I   (C) G   (D) C

21   Who is fourth to the left of H?

(A) J   (B) A   (C) B   (C) K

22.   Who is fifth to the right of B?

(A) E   (B) A   (C) H   (D) D

9
Chapter

Objective ///

- To unravel mathematical puzzles through reasoning, observation and substitution.

- To trace out numerals following certain conditions.

  In these type of questions a figure or a matrix is given in which some numbers are filled according to a rule. A place is left blank. The candidate has to find out a number from the given possible answers which may be filled in the blank space.

Example 1

Which number will replace the question mark?

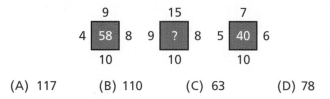

(A) 117	(B) 110	(C) 63	(D) 78

Answer: (D)

Explanation:

Rule: The central number is the difference of the products of the opposite numers.

In the 1st figure: $(9 \times 10) - (8 \times 4) = 90 - 32 = 58$

In the 3rd figure: $(7 \times 10) - (5 \times 6) = 70 - 30 = 40$

Similarly, in the 2nd figure: $(15 \times 10) - (9 \times 8) = 150 - 72 = 78$

REASONING TRAINER Plus

Example 2

Find the missing number.

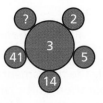

(A) 122   (B) 123   (C) 124   (D) 112

Answer: (A)

Explanation:

Rule:

$(2 \times 3) - 1 = 5$

$(5 \times 3) - 1 = 14$

$(14 \times 3) - 1 = 41$

Similarly $41 \times 3 - 1 = 122$

Example 3

Find the missing number.

3 C	2 B	4 A
27 A	?	64 B
9 C	4 A	16 B

(A) 18 C   (B) 16 C   (C) 8 C   (D) 12 B

Answer: (C)

Explanation:

Rule: In each row, out of the letters A, B and C, each must appear once.

43

In each column, the product of first and third number is equal to second number.

So, the missing number will be (2 × 4) = 8 and the missing letter will be C.

Hence the required pair is 8 C.

Mathematical Operations

This concept deals with questions on simple mathematical operations. Generally the fundamental operations like addition, subtraction, multiplication and divisions are represented by symbols, different from the usual ones. Sometimes artificial symbols can also be used. A student has to substitute the usual signs and solve the questions accordingly, to get the correct answer.

Note: While solving a mathematical expression, we must follow the BODMAS rule.

i.e., Brackets → Of → Division → Multiplication → Addition → Subtraction.

e.g., $(46 - 24) \div 11 + 6 \div 2 - 1 = 22 \div 11 + 6 \div 2 - 1$ (Solving bracket)

$$= 2 + 3 - 1 \quad \text{(Division)}$$
$$= 5 - 1 \quad \text{(Addition)}$$
$$= 4 \quad \text{(Subtraction)}$$

Example 4

If + means x, x means -, - means ÷ and ÷ means +, then which of the options gives the result of 175 - 25 ÷ 5 + 20 x 3 + 10?

(A) 57   (B) 77   (C) 240   (D) 2370

Answer: (B)

Explanation:

Step ①

Replace the signs as given in condition.

Required expression = $(175 \div 25 + 5 \times 20 - 3 \times 10)$

Step (2)

Apply BODMAS rule and solve.

$175 \div 25 + 5 \times 20 - 3 \times 10$

$= 7 + 5 \times 20 - 3 \times 10$ ($\because 175 \div 25 = 7$) - (Division)

$= 7 + 100 - 30$ ($\because 5 \times 20 = 100; 3 \times 10 = 30$) (Multiplication)

$= 107 - 30$ ($\because 7 + 100 = 107$ (Addition)

$= 77$ ($\because 107 - 30 = 77$) (Subtraction)

Example 5

If L stands for +, M stands for -, N stands for x and P stands for $\div$ then what is the value of 14N10L42P2M8?

(A) 153   (B) 216   (C) 248   (D) 251

Answer: (A)

Explanation:

Step 1:

Replace the signs as given in the condition.

$\therefore$ Required expression = $14 \times 10 + 42 \div 2 - 8$

Step 2:

Apply BODMAS rule and solve.

$14 \times 10 + 42 \div 2 - 8$

$= 14 \times 10 + 21 - 8$ ($\because 42 \div 2 = 21$) (Division)

$= 140 + 21 - 8$ ($\because 14 \times 10 = 140$) (Multiplication)

$= 161 - 8$ ($\because 140 + 21 = 161$) (Addition)

$= 153$ ($\because 161 - 8 = 153$) (Subtraction)

$\therefore$ Answer is option (A).

Example 6

If 'a' means ' ÷ ', 'b' means 'x', 'c' means '+' and 'd' means '-' then what is the value of 48c5d16b8a4?

(A) 13   (B) 19   (C) 21   (D) 45

Answer: (C)

Explanation:

Step ①

Replace the signs as given in the condition.

∴ Required expression = 48 + 5 - 16 x 8 ÷ 4

Step ②

Apply BODMAS rule and solve.

48 + 5 - 16 x 8 ÷ 4

= 48 + 5 - 16 x 2   (∵ 8 ÷ 4 = 2) (Division)

= 48 + 5 - 32   (∵ 16 x 2 = 32) (Multiplication)

= 53 - 32   (∵ 48 + 5 = 53) (Addition)

= 21   (∵ 53 - 32 = 21) (Subtraction)

Example 7

If ⬜ stands for +, ⬜ stands for - , ⬜ stands for x and ⬜ stands for ÷ , then find the value of 30 ⬜ 54 ⬜ (20 ⬜ 5 ⬜ 2).

(A) 17   (B) 20   (C) 24   (D) 28

Answer: (A)

Explanation:

Step ①

Replace the signs as given in the condition.

∴ Required expression = 30 - 5 + 4 x (20 ÷ 5 - 2)

Step ②

Apply BODMAS rule and solve.

30 - 5 + 4 x [20 ÷ 5 - 2]

= 30 - 5 + 4 x [4 - 2] (∵ 20 ÷ 5 = 4) (Division in bracket)

= 30 - 5 + 4 x 2   (∵ 4 - 2 = 2) (Bracket)

= 30 - 5 + 8   (∵ 4 x 2 = 8) (Multiplication)

= 30 - 13   (∵ 5 + 8 = 13) (Addition)

= 17   (∵ 30 - 13 = 7) (Subtraction)

Example 8

If $7 * 1 = 64$, $3 * 9 = 144$, $5 * 3 = 64$, then what is the value of $6 * 5$?

(A) 144   (B) 121   (C) 96   (D) 78

Answer: (B)

Explanation:

The rule which is applicable here is,

$x * y = (x + y) \times (x + y)$

Since, $7 * 1 = (7 + 1) \times (7 + 1) = 8 \times 8 = 64$

$3 * 9 = (3 + 9) \times (3 + 9) = 12 \times 12 = 144$

$5 * 3 = (5 + 3) \times (5 + 3) = 8 \times 8 = 64$

In the a same way,

$6 * 5 = (6 + 5) \times (6 + 5) = 11 \times 11 = 121$

TRY THESE

1. Which number will replace the question mark in the following?

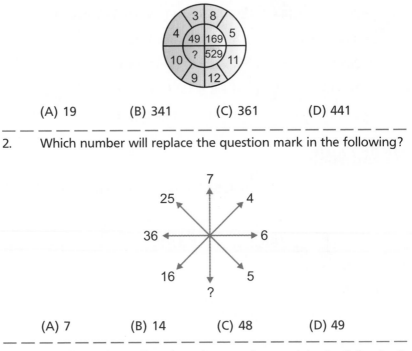

(A) 19　　　　(B) 341　　　　(C) 361　　　　(D) 441

2. Which number will replace the question mark in the following?

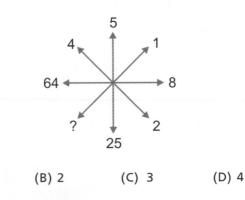

(A) 7　　　　(B) 14　　　　(C) 48　　　　(D) 49

3. Which number will replace the question mark in the following?

5
4　　　1
64 ←　　　→ 8
?　　　2
25

(A) 1　　　　(B) 2　　　　(C) 3　　　　(D) 4

4. Which number will replace the question mark in the following?

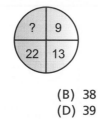

(A) 40   (B) 38
(C) 44   (D) 39

5. Which number will replace the question mark?

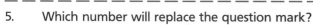

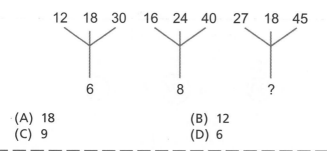

(A) 9   (B) 21
(C) 11   (D) 10

6. Which number will replace the question mark in the following?

(A) 18   (B) 12
(C) 9   (D) 6

7. Which number will replace the question mark?

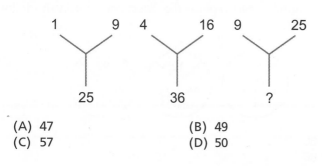

(A) 47   (B) 49
(C) 57   (D) 50

49

8. Which number will replace the question mark in the following?

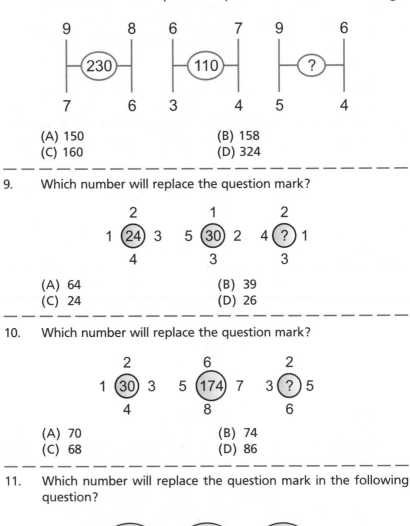

(A) 150   (B) 158
(C) 160   (D) 324

9. Which number will replace the question mark?

    2   1   2
1 (24) 3   5 (30) 2   4 (?) 1
    4   3   3

(A) 64   (B) 39
(C) 24   (D) 26

10. Which number will replace the question mark?

    2   6   2
1 (30) 3   5 (174) 7   3 (?) 5
    4   8   6

(A) 70   (B) 74
(C) 68   (D) 86

11. Which number will replace the question mark in the following question?

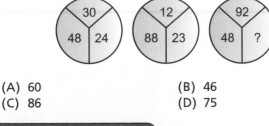

(A) 60   (B) 46
(C) 86   (D) 75

REASONING TRAINER Plus

12. Which number will replace the question mark?

(A) 8   (B) 14   (C) 10   (D) 6

Directions for 13 to 18: If '+' is 'x', '−' is '+', 'x' is ' ÷ ' and ' ÷ ' is '−', then answer the following questions based on the information.

13. $21 \div 8 + 2 - 12 \times 3 = ?$

(A) 14   (B) 9   (C) 13.5   (D) 11

14. $15 \times 5 \div 3 + 1 - 1 = ?$

(A) − 1   (B) − 2   (C) 3   (D) 1

15. $6 - 9 + 8 \times 3 \div 20 = ?$

(A) − 2   (B) 6   (C) 10   (D) 12

16. $6 + 7 \times 3 - 8 \div 20 = ?$

(A) − 3   (B) 7   (C) 2   (D) 1

17. $9 - 3 + 2 \div 16 \times 2 = ?$

(A) 7   (B) 5   (C) 9   (D) 6

18. $3 \times 2 + 4 - 2 \div 9 = ?$

(A) − 1   (B) 1   (C) − 2   (D) 3

19. If 10×2 means $5, 10 \div 4$ means 14, $10 + 4$ means 6 and $10 - 4$ means 40 then $10 \times 5 \div 4 + 3 - 2 = ?$

(A) 4   (B) 0   (C) 15   (D) 2

20. If $40 + 10 = 30$, $18 + 8 = 10$, then $60 + 60 = ?$

(A) 120   (B) 3600   (C) 0   (D) 90

21. If '+' means '−' ; '−' means 'x', 'x' means '÷' and '÷' means '+', then 2 ÷ 6 x 6 ÷ 2 = ?

    (A) 1   (B) 0   (C) 5   (D) 6

22. If 7 * 1 = 65; 3 * 9 = 114

    What is the value of 5 * 6?

    (A) 22   (B) 55   (C) 66   (D) 121

23. If 60 x 3 = 36; 11 x 7 = 81, then

    What is the value of 5 x 13?

    (A) 65   (B) 66   (C) 81   (D) 51

Directions for 24 to 26: In the statement below, two signs in the equations given have been interchanged. Final out these two signs to make the equations correct.

24. 6 x 4 + 2 = 26

    (A) + and x, 2 and 4   (B) + and x, 4 and 6
    (C) + and x, 2 and 6   (D) None of these

25. 3 ÷ 5 x 8 + 2 − 10 = 13

    (A) + and −   (B) x and ÷   (C) ÷ and −   (D) ÷ and +

26. 51 ÷ 3 + 17 x 2 − 12 = 10

    (A) + and ÷   (B) − and x   (C) ÷ and x   (D) x and +

27. If x stands for 'add', y stands for 'subtract', z stands for 'divide' and P stands for 'multiply, then what is the value of (7P3) y 6 x 5?

    (A) 5   (B) 10   (C) 15   (D) 20

Objective

To judge a candidate's ability to decipher the pattern which goes behind a coded message or statement.

A 'code' is a system of conveying a message through signals. It is a method of sending a message between a sender and a receiver in such a way that only the sender and the receiver know its meaning. Coding is done according to a certain pattern in the mind of the sender. So its meaning cannot be deciphered by a third person unless he carefully studies the pattern.This process is called decoding.

In coding generally artificial values are assigned to certain given words and the candidates are required to find out the code for another given word.

Example 1

If RAM is coded as QZL in a certain language, then how will LAMP be coded in that language?

(A) KZLO   (B) MBNQ   (C) KZLP   (D) KLZN

Answer: (A)

Explanation:

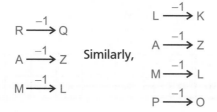

$\therefore$ Code of LAMP is KZLO.

Example 2

If ROAST is coded as PQYUR in a certain language, then how will SLOPPY be coded in that language?

(A) MRNAQN (B) NRMNQA (C) QNMRNA (D) RANNMQ

Answer: (C)

Explanation:

Clearly, the letters in the word ROAST are moved alternately two steps backward and two steps forward to obtain the letters of the code. Thus, we have:

$$\begin{array}{ccccc} R & O & A & S & T \\ -2\downarrow & +2\downarrow & -2\downarrow & +2\downarrow & -2\downarrow \\ P & Q & Y & U & R \end{array}$$

Similarly,

$$\begin{array}{cccccc} S & L & O & P & P & Y \\ -2\downarrow & +2\downarrow & -2\downarrow & +2\downarrow & -2\downarrow & +2\downarrow \\ Q & N & M & R & N & A \end{array}$$

So, the required code is QNMRNA. Hence, the answer is (C).

Example 3

If in a certain code 24657 is written as BPSIN and 1893 as KMLX then which number will be written as PINXS?

(A) 24897   (B) 45736   (C) 45637   (D) 45763

Answer: (B)

Explanation:

2	4	6	5	7
B	P	S	I	N

and

1	8	9	3
K	M	L	X

From both the tables, PINXS = 45736

Example 4

If TEMPLE is coded as VHQURL, how would you code CHURCH?

(A) EKYWIO   (B) EKUWIO   (C) EKYWIN   (D) EKYWJO

Answer: (A)

Explanation:

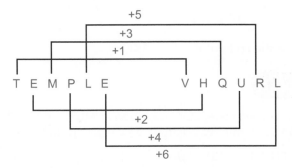

Code for T is V, for E it is H, for M it is Q. It may be noticed from here that letters of TEMPLE have been replaced by new letters from the alphabets.

There is a gap of one letter between T and V, a gap of two letters between E and H, a gap of three letters between M and Q and so on in the alphabets.

Therefore, coding for CHURCH is

C	H	U	R	C	H
+1	+2	+3	+4	+5	+6
E	K	Y	W	I	O

Hence, (A) is the correct answer.

Example 5

What is the code of BARKS,

If MARCH is coded as HCRAM?

(A) BASKR   (B) CBSLT   (C) SKRAB   (D) SRKAB

Answer: (C)

Explanation:

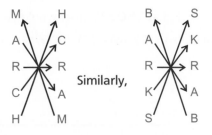

Similarly,

Hence the code of BARKS is SKRAB.

Example 6

If in a certain code, LUTE is written as MUTE and FATE is written as GATE, then how will BLUE be written in that code?

(A) CLUE   (B) GLUE   (C) FLUE   (D) SLUE

Answer: (A)

Explanation:

The first letter of the word is moved one step forward to obtain the first letter of the code, while the other letters remain unaltered.

Hence, BLUE will be written as CLUE.

Example 7

Read the information given below, and answer the questions that follow.

In a certain code "rem tur dimi wee" means "my pencil was stolen", "soz rem legh ner" means "your pencil is here", "rem zet tur legh" means "blue pencil was here" and "dimi rem tur soz" means "your pencil was stolen".

i. Which of the following is the code for the word "here"?

(A) tur   (B) ner   (C) dimi   (D) legh

Answer: (D)

Explanation:

1. "rem tur dimi wee" ⇒ "my pencil was stolen".

2. "soz rem legh ner" ⇒ "your pencil is here".

3. "rem zet tur legh" ⇒ "blue pencil was here".

4. "dimi rem tur soz" ⇒ "your pencil was stolen".

Thus from (2) & (3), we get "rem legh" ⇒ pencil here" (though not necessarily in the same order). Further, from (1), (2), (3) & (4) together, we get "rem" = "pencil". Hence, we get, "legh" = "here".

ii. Which of the following indicates "blue pencil is stolen"?

(A) Zet rem ner dimi   (B) Ner legh tur zut
(C) Dimi rem soz ner   (D) Zet legh tur rem

Answer: (A)

Explanation:

We have, "rem" = "pencil". Now from (3) & (4),

we get "tur" = "was" and

since "legh" = "ere", we get, "zet" = "blue".

Now, from (1) & (4), we get, "rem tur dimi" = "pencil was stolen". Hence, we get "dimi" = "stolen".

Now, from (4), we get,

"soz" = "your". Hence, from (2), we get, "ner" = "is".

Thus, "zet rem ner dimi" = "blue pencil is stolen".

Example 8

In a certain code language,

i. 'pit na sa' means 'you are welcome';

ii. 'na ho pa la' means 'they are very good';

iii. 'ka da la' means 'who is good';

iv. 'od ho pit la' means 'they welcome good people';

57

1. Which of the following means 'people' in that code language?

   (A) od   (B) la   (C) ho   (D) pit

2. Which of the following means 'very' in that code language?

   (A) pa   (B) na
   (C) da   (D) Data inadequate

Answer: 1 (A)

Explanation:

1. In statements (i) and (iv), the common code word is 'pit' and the common word is 'welcome'. So, 'pit' means 'welcome'.

   In statements (ii) and (iv), the common code - words are 'ho' and 'la' and the common words are 'they' and 'good'. So, 'ho' and 'la' mean 'they' and 'good'. Thus, in (iv), the remaining code - word i.e. 'od' means 'people'.

   Hence, the answer is (A).

Answer: 2 (A)

Explanation:

   From 1, we know that 'ho' and 'la' are codes for 'they' and 'good'.

   Now, in statements (i) and (ii), the common code - word is 'na' and the common word is 'are'. So, 'na' means 'are'.

   Thus, in (ii), the remaining code - word i.e. 'pa' means 'very'.

   Hence, the answer is (A).

Example 9

   If E = 5, PEN = 35, then PAGE = ?

   (A) 27   (B) 28   (C) 29   (D) 36

Answer: (C)

Explanation:

   Clearly, putting A = 1, B = 2, C = 3, D = 4, E = 5, ..., M = 13, ..., X = 25, Z = 26, we have:

   PEN = P + E + N = 16 + 5 + 14 = 35.

   So, PAGE = P + A + G + E = 16 + 1 + 7 + 5 = 29.

   Hence, the answer is (C).

TRY THESE

1. In a certain code, INSTITUTION is written as NOITUTITSNI. How is PERFECTION written in that code?

   (A) NOICTEFREP   (B) NOITCEFERP
   (C) NOITCEFRPE   (D) NOITCEFREP

2. In a certain code, GOODNESS is coded as HNPCODTR. How is GREATNESS coded in that code?

   (A) HQFZUODTR   (B) HQFZUMFRT
   (C) HQFZSMFRT   (D) FSDBSODTR

3. If ROSE is coded as 6821, CHAIR is coded as 73456 and PREACH is coded as 961473, what will be the code for SEARCH?

   (A) 246173   (B) 214673
   (C) 214763   (D) 216473

Directions for 4 to 6: The table below gives the codes for consonants of the English alphabet.

Letters	G	B	K	H	Z	M	F
	R	V	C	S	D	Q	X
	J	N	T	L	W	Y	P
Digits	5	4	1	3	2	8	7

i. Letters of the English alphabet are coded by the digits from 1 to 8. Vowels are coded either by other digits or by $.

ii. If any vowel is neither at the first place nor at the last place of the word then it is coded as '6'

iii. If any vowel is either at the first or at the last place of the word then it is coded as '9'.

iv. If the same vowel is at the first and at the last place of the word then it is coded as '$'.

Applying these conditions find the right code in each question.

4. Find the code of PKDEJHI.

   (A) 712653$ (B) 7129539
   (C) 7126539   (D) 712 $ 53 $

5. Find the code of OPTIONAL.

   (A) $7166463   (B) $7199493
   (C) 67199493   (D) 97166463

6. Find the code of EGTARLQE.

   (A) 95165389   (B) 65195386
   (C) $ 517538 $ (D) $ 516538 $

7. If in a certain code 56431 is written as RSHTU and 98270 as MLKPA then how will 9517 be written in the same code?

   (A) MRUP   (B) MURP   (C) MRPU   (D) MRPT

8. If in a certain code 19078 is written as JPHSX and 65432 as DBAIK then how will 89235 be written in the same code?

   (A) JPDBI   (B) XHVSK   (D) HPJAK   (D) XPKIB

9. If in a certain code 65312 is written as NOSRP and 7894 as VTMA then how will 3476 be written in the same code?

   (A) SAVN   (B) SANV   (C) SNAV   (D) SNVA

10. If GARIMA is coded as 725432 and TINA as 6482, how will MARTINA be coded?

   (A) 3256482   (B) 3265842   (C) 3645862   (D) 3658426

Directions for 11 to 15: Use the table given and answer the questions following it.

A	B	C	D	E	F	G	H	I	J	K	L	M	N	O	P	Q	R	S	T	U	V	W	X	Y	Z
u	a	2	v	b	w	3	t	4	x	s	y	5	z	6	c	d	8	7	e	r	h	9	i	p	q

11. If DASH is coded as 2 a 8 4, then what is the code of SMASH in that language?

   (A) 75 U 7 t   (B) e y a 8 4   (C) 8 z q e 3   (D) 8 z q e 4

12. If FASHION is coded as z64t7uw, then find the code of POSITION.

   (A) z64e476c   (B) z64e47c6   (C) c674e46z   (D) c674e4z6

13. If MAIDEN is u5v4zb, then find the code of DANGER.

   (A) vuz3b8   (B) 8b3zuv   (C) uv3z8b   (D) uv3zb8

14.   If MAY is yzqaiq, then find the code of TIE.

(A) 7rtxwv   (B) 7rtxvw   (C) 7rtxbw   (D) 7rtxwb

15.   If LONDON is 5c62z5, then find the code of EUROPE.

(A) wh7cdw   (B) wh7z6w   (C) br76cb   (D) wh76cb

16.   If in a certain code, GLAMOUR is written as INCOQWT and MISRULE is written as OKUTWNG, then how will TOPICAL be written in that code?

(A) VMRJECN   (B) VMRHACJ
(C) RFKFNP   (D) VQRKECN

17.   In a certain code, INACTIVE is written as VITCANIE. How will COMPUTER be written in the same code?

(A) PMOCRETU   (B) ETUPMOCR
(C) UTEPMOCR   (D) RETRUPMOC

18.   If DELHI can be coded as CCIDD, then how would you code BOMBAY?

(A) AJMTVT   (B) AMJXVS   (C) MJXVSU   (D) WXYZAX

19.   In a certain language, SIGHT is written as VLJKW. How is REVEAL written in the same language?

(A) UHYHDO   (B) ODHYHU   (C) FSJSOZ   (D) UHYHDL

_ _

Directions for 20 to 23: In a certain code, letters of the English alphabet (consonants and vowels) are coded as given for some words below. The numeric code for each letter is given in bracket under coded form and corresponds to the letter in the word in the same serial order. Study the coded forms of the given words and find out the rules for their codification. Applying those rules, answer the questions that follow.

Word	Coded Form
SEAT	[5] [15] [15] [15]
CUT	[5] [10] [5]
ONE	[0] [5] [0]
DEEP	[5] [20] [20] [5]
POUR	[5] [15] [15] [5]

61

© *Brain Mapping Academy*

PIN	[5] [10] [5]
NONE	[5] [25] [5] [25]
BOOK	[5] [20] [20] [5]
OPEN	[30] [5] [30] [5]
ATE	[0] [5] [0]
PAGE	[5] [25] [5] [25]
UNIT	[30] [5] [30] [5]

Find out the coded form of each of the words.

20. DOSE

(A) [5] [15] [5] [15]   (B) [5] [10] [5] [10]
(C) [5] [30] [5] [30]   (D) [5] [25] [5] [25]

21. AGED

(A) [0] [5] [0] [5]   (B) [30] [10] [30] [10]
(C) [30] [5] [30] [5]   (D) [25] [5] [25] [5]

22. DATA

(A) [5] [30] [5] [30]   (B) [5] [25] [5] [25]
(C) [5] [15] [5] [15]   (D) [5] [10] [5] [10]

23. EVE

(A) [0] [5] [0]   (B) [0] [15] [0]
(C) [15] [5] [15]   (D) [0] [10] [10]

24. In a certain code language '389' means 'run very fast'. '964' means 'come back fast' and '487' means 'run and come'. Which digit in the language means 'come'?

(A) 7   (B) 9   (C) 4   (D) 8

25. If 'nitco sco tingo' means 'softer than flower'; 'tingo rho mst' means 'sweet flower fragrance' and 'mst sco tmp' means 'sweet than smile'. What would 'fragrance' stand for in that language?

(A) rho   (B) mst   (C) tmp   (D) sco

26. If GOLD is coded as HOMD, COME is coded as DONE and CORD is coded as DOSD, how would you code SONS?

(A) TPOT   (B) TOOT   (C) TOOS   (D) TONT

REASONING TRAINER Plus

27. In a certain code language, 'col tip mot' means 'singing is appreciable', 'mot baj min' means 'dancing is good' and 'tip mop baj' means 'singing and dancing. Which of the following means 'good' in that code language?

(A) mot   (B) min
(C) baj   (D) col

28. If in a certain language, 'oka peru' means 'fine cloth'; 'lisa pani' means 'clear water' and 'dona lisa peru' means 'fine clear weather', which word in that language means 'weather'?

(A) oka   (B) peru   (C) lisa   (D) dona

29. In a certain code language 'si po re' means 'book is thick', 'ti' na 're' means 'bag is heavy', 'ka si' means 'interesting book' and 'de ti' means 'that bag'. Which of the following means 'that is interesting' in that code language?

(A) ka re na   (B) de si re
(C) ti po ka   (D) ka de re

30. In a certain coded language, 'pick and choose' is written as 'ko ho po' and 'pick up and come' is written as 'to no ko po'. How is 'pick' written in that code?

(A) ko   (B) po
(C) Either ko or po   (D) Cannot be determined

Chapters like Which one is different, Analogy and What comes next comes under this category.

Let us study some common properties before learning those chapters.

1. Manipulation:

In non-verbal reasoning, shapes can be manipulated by:

A. Size   B. Transformation   C. Addition

D. Subtraction   E. Frequency

A. Shapes can increase in size or decrease in size.

(i) Enlargement   (ii) Reduction

Transformation:

Shapes can be transformed. This means a shape can be stretched or squashed, but retains its main characteristics i.e., the same number of sides and vertices (corners) and one dimension must remain constant.

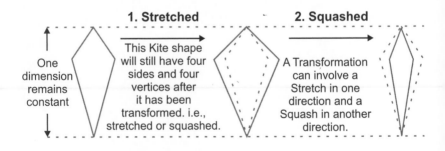

1. Stretched

2. Squashed

One dimension remains constant

This Kite shape will still have four sides and four vertices after it has been transformed. i.e., stretched or squashed.

A Transformation can involve a Stretch in one direction and a Squash in another direction.

Addition:

One or more shapes can be added to the original shape or separate additional shape can be added for example.

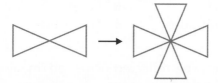

The original shape has been copied, rotated 90° and superimposed onto the original shape. Additions are often combined with rotations, reflections, superimpositions and inversions.

Subtraction:

Shapes or parts of a shape can be subtracted from the original shape or shapes. For example:

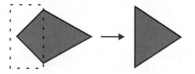

The original kite shape with a grey fill has a triangular section subtracted from it [as marked in the figure above]. The shape that remains is an isosceles triangle with a grey fill.

Frequency (Counting):

Frequency involves the counting of shapes, small shapes within other shapes, or parts of shapes.

(i) Counting shapes

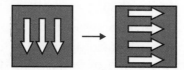

The original shape has three vertical arrows. The frequency (number) in the second shape is increased to four horizontal arrows. This change could also be understood as an addition.

Movement:

In non - verbal reasoning, shapes move in these ways. They can

A. Reflect   B. Rotate   C. Invert

D. Superimpose   E. Transpose

Reflections:

A shape can be reflected across an imaginary mirror line or line of reflection.

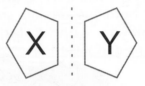

Shape X is reflected on the other side of the mirror line to form shape Y.

Rotation:

In non - verbal reasoning, shapes can rotate in clockwise or anti-clockwise direction. To avoid confusion, it is best to measure the rotation by the shortest route. This will be either in a clockwise or an anti-clockwise direction around the 360° turn.

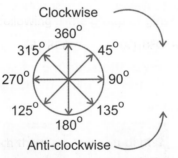

Smaller shapes can rotate around the outside of larger shapes or on the inside of larger shapes.

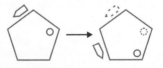

The pencil shape has moved anti - clockwise around the pentagon shape and the circle shape has moved clockwise within the pentagon shape.

Inversions:

In non - verbal reasoning, a shape can be inverted (flipped) horizontally or vertically or in both directions at the same time.

Vertical Inversion/Flip:

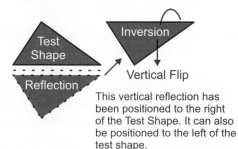

This vertical reflection has been positioned to the right of the Test Shape. It also can be positioned to the left of the test shape.

Vertical inversion or flip: It can be understood as a vertical reflection positioned to the right or left side of the original shape. It can also be seen as a vertical flip.

Horizontal Inversion/Flip:

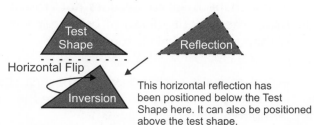

This horizontal reflection has been positioned below the Test Shape here. It can also be positioned above the test shape.

Horizontal inversion: This can be understood as a horizontal reflection positioned underneath or above the original shape. It can also be seen as a horizontal flip.

Vertical and Horizontal Inversion/Double Flip:

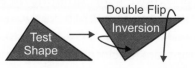

© Brain Mapping Academy

Combined vertical and horizontal inversion or flip: This is 180° rotation of the original shape.

Superimposition:

In non - verbal reasoning, shapes can be superimposed onto other shapes. These superimpositions can include a Merger, an Overlay, A linkage or an Enclosure.

Superimpositions can be indicated with a grey fill to help with visual clarity and ease of understanding.

Merger:

The second shape merges (crosses over) the first shape. The integrity (lines) of both shapes are retained. In this case it is a 90° rotation and inversion of the original shape.

Overlay:

The second shape overlays (is on top of) the first shape. The original shape is partially covered. In this case it is a 90° rotation of the original shape.

Linkage:

The second shape is linked to (does not cross over) the first shape. The integrity (lines) of both shapes are kept. Several shapes can be linked together.

Enclosure:

The second shape is enclosed within the first shape. In this case a copy of the first shape is reduced in size and enclosed within the original shape.

Transposition:

In non - verbal reasoning, shapes can be transposed or moved from one position to another, either horizontally or vertically. Movement to the right or to the left are horizontal and movements up or down are vertical. Some transpositions involve both vertical and horizontal movements i.e., a shape could move up and to the right. Transpositions are enclosed to show movement.

1. Horizontal transpositon   2. Vertical transpositon
3. Horizontal and vertical transpositon

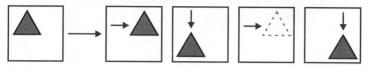

Patterns:

Shapes can make patterns in two ways.

A. Repetition   B. Cumulation

Repetitive:

Shapes can be arranged in a repetitive patterns.

The telegraph poles are in a repetitive pattern of one, two, three, two, one, two, three crossbars etc.

Cumulative:

Shapes can be arranged in a cumulative pattern.

The pentagon shape builds line by line in five stages.

Layering:

Non - verbal reasoning questions are complicated by the process of layering. Questions can have up to five layers (or changes) that have to be observed, to find a solution. Some shapes only have one layer or change.

The segment shape has only received one layer or change. It has been rotated 180°.

WHICH ONE IS DIFFERENT ?

Objective ///

- To sharpen your ability to distinguish shapes or symbols according to their common features.

- To test your ability to find shapes that are similar or different.

  The question types we will look at in this section are often referred to as 'Similarities questions'. They test your ability to work out which shapes are similar and which are different in a given set of options.

  You need to use your observation skills to compare the given shapes and symbols and find the visual link or links.

  Questions on odd one out are generally from the types given below.

  In verbal reasoning, numbers/letters are joined with certain mathematical rules.

  In non-verbal reasoning, we should consider the following factors before solving problems.

  Shapes, positions, lines, movements, additions, subtractions, countings, repetition etc.

Example 1

Which is the odd one out?

(A) □⟶   (B) ↑   (C) ↓   (D) ↓

Answer: (C)

Explanation:

A quick look at the given symbols reveals that all of them are similar. We need to take a closer look to identify a feature that separates one of the given symbols from the remaining three.

Let us identify the required feature in the given figures.

- Each symbol is made up of an arrow and a square; so the feature cannot be the shape.

- Each arrow is shaded cyan and each square is white fill; the feature cannot be the shading.

- The square is on the left-hand side of some arrows and on the right-hand side of others; the feature cannot be the position.

What else could be different in one of these options?

Working from left to right, break each symbol down and look at the two shapes individually.

1. The square in option A is of the same size as the squares in B, C and D. This cannot be used to identify the odd one out.

2. The arrow in option A is of the same length as the arrows in each of the other symbols. This will not lead us to identify the feature.

3. The arrowhead in option A is:

- Of the same size as the arrowhead in B. (A) ⟶ ↑ (B)

- Larger than the arrowhead in C. (A) ⟶ ↓ (C)

- The same size as the arrowhead in D. (A) ⟶ ↓ (D)

Have we found a common feature that is shared by four options? Yes, the arrowheads in A, B and D are all the same size. Symbol C has a smaller arrowhead so this must be the odd one out.

Example 2

Find the figure which is different from the others.

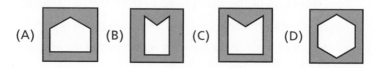

Answer: (D)

Explanation:

All the figures are made up of five lines but the figure (D) is made up of six lines. Hence (D) is different from the others.

Example 3

Find the odd one out.

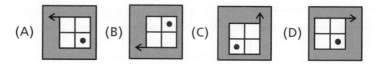

Answer: (D)

Explanation:

In all the figures except (D) the arrow and the black dot are diagonally in opposite squares. In option (D), they are in the adjacent (nearer) squares. Hence, the odd figure is (D).

Example 4

Which is different from the others?

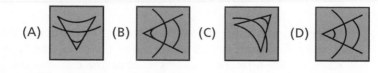

Answer: (B)

Explanation:

In all the figures, except (B), all the curved lines have curves in the same direction. In option (B), the upper curve is in opposite direction and hence, does not belong to this group. Therefore the odd figure is (B).

Example 5

Which figure is different from the others?

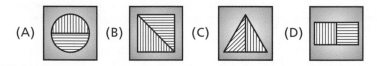

Answer: (C)

Explanation:

In each of the figures, except (C), one - half of the figure has horizontal shading. Hence, the odd figure is option (C).

Example 6

Find the odd one out.

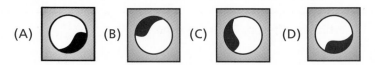

Answer: (D)

Explanation:

In this case, all the figures, except (D) can be rotated into each other. Hence, the odd figure is (D).

TRY THESE

1. Find the odd one out.

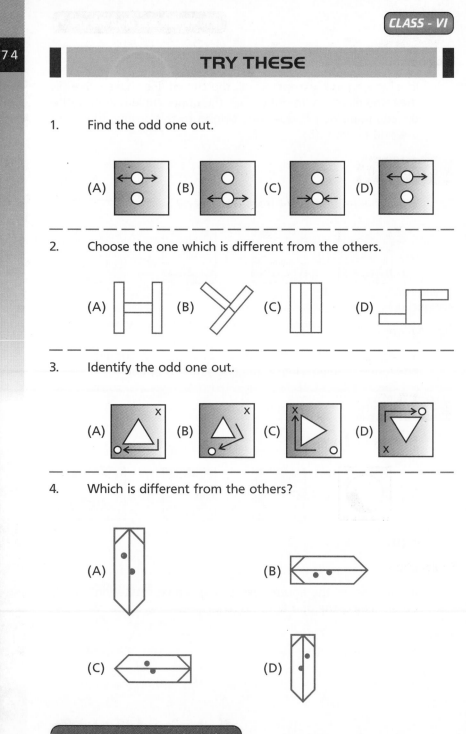

2. Choose the one which is different from the others.

3. Identify the odd one out.

4. Which is different from the others?

5. Which is the odd one out?

(A) J (B) F (C) M (D) A

6. Find the odd one out.

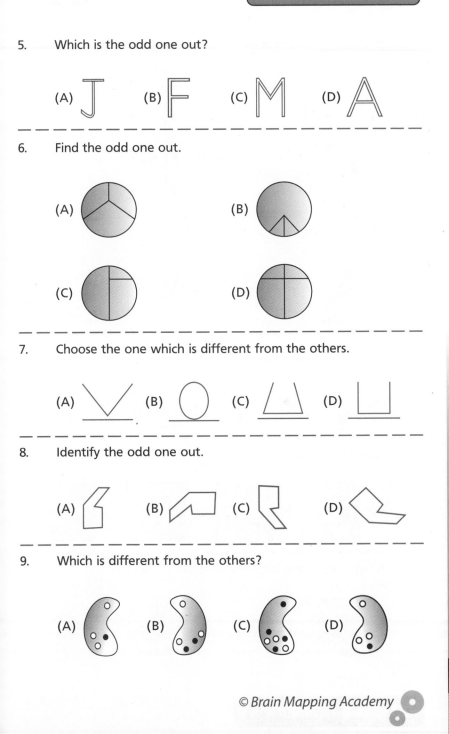

(A)

(B)

(C)

(D)

7. Choose the one which is different from the others.

(A) V (B) O (C) △ (D) ⊔

8. Identify the odd one out.

(A) (B) (C) (D)

9. Which is different from the others?

(A) (B) (C) (D)

10. Which is the odd one out?

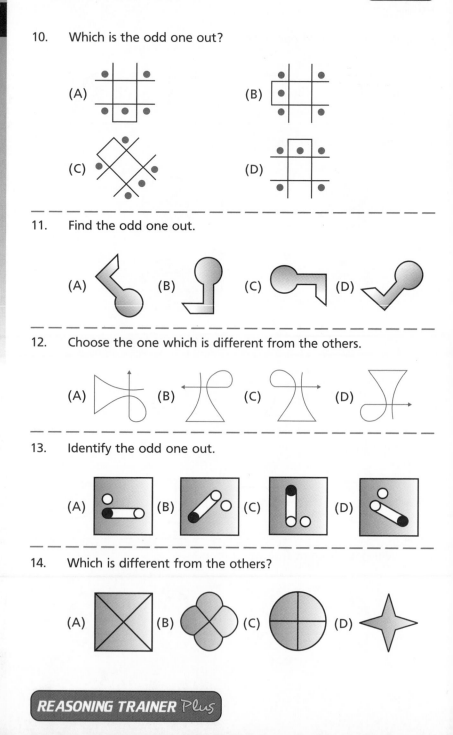

(A)

(B)

(C)

(D)

11. Find the odd one out.

(A)　　　(B)　　　(C)　　　(D)

12. Choose the one which is different from the others.

(A)　　　(B)　　　(C)　　　(D)

13. Identify the odd one out.

(A)　　(B)　　(C)　　(D)

14. Which is different from the others?

(A)　　(B)　　(C)　　(D)

15.   Which is the odd one out?

(A) (B) (C) (D)

16.   Find the odd one out.

(A)   (B)

(C)   (D)

17.   Choose the one which is different from the others.

(A)   (B)

(C)   (D)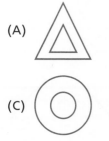

18.   Identify the odd one out.

(A)   (B)

(C)   (D)

19. Which is different from the others?

(A)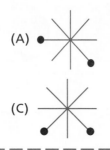

(B)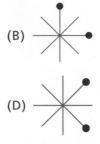

(C)

(D)

20. Which is the odd one out?

(A)

(B)

(C)

(D)

21. Find the odd one out.

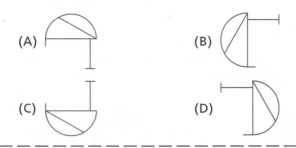

(A)

(B)

(C)

(D)

22. Choose the one which is different from the others.

(A)   (B)   (C)   (D)

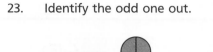

23. Identify the odd one out.

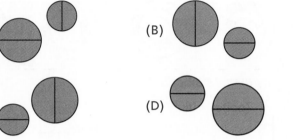

(A)

(B)

(C)

(D)

24. Which is different from the others?

(A)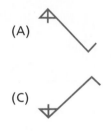

(B)

(C)

(D)

25. Which is the odd one out?

(A)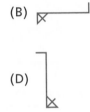

(B)

(C)

(D)

26. Find the odd one out.

(A) (B): (C)  (D)

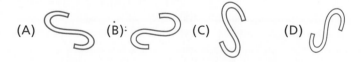

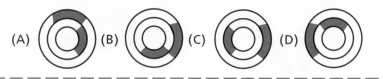

27. Choose the one which is different from the others.

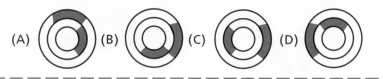

(A)   (B)   (C)   (D)

28. Identify the odd one out.

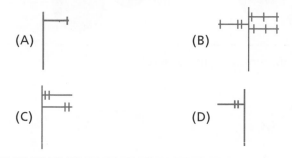

(A)   (B)

(C)   (D)

29. Which is different from the others?

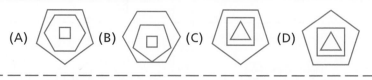

(A)   (B)   (C)   (D)

30. Which is the odd one out?

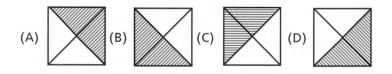

(A)   (B)   (C)   (D)

ANALOGY

Objective ///

- To enable the student to find a connecting link between two different factors.

  In both verbal and non - verbal reasoning, analogy questions test your ability to spot a connection between two concepts.

  You will usually be given one pair of images that are connected in a particular way. You have to find the correct image to complete the second pair in the same way as the first pair.

  As with the similarities group, analogies can be based on a variety of different connections.

  Let's start with some straight forward examples.

Example 1

Which shape or pattern completes the second pair in the same way as the first pair?

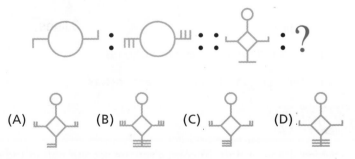

Answer: (B)

Explanation:

A quick look at the first pair of objects shows that:

- They are of the same shape.
- They are of the same size.
- They are in the same position.
- The thickness of the lines is the same.

None of these elements can form the link between the objects. So what connection can you see between the two shapes?

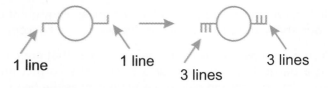

1 line   1 line   3 lines

3 lines

The connection between these two shapes is related to number; each short single line in the first symbol has become three short lines in the second symbol.

Now you can use this analogy to predict the symbol that will complete the second pair.

1 line   1 line   3 lines   3 lines

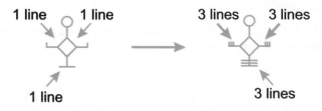

1 line   3 lines

This predicted symbol matches option B.

Therefore, option (B) is the correct answer.

Example 2

Which shape or pattern completes the second pair in the same way as the first pair?

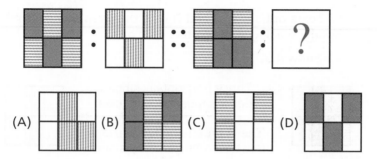

Answer: (A)

Explanation:

> You should be able to see quite quickly that the connection for this analogy question relates to shading.
>
> Before you look at exactly how the shading is different, make sure that there are no other differences between the first pair. In this example, the objects are:

- of the same shape.

- of the same size.

- split into the same number of sections.

- in the same position.

> So, let us look more closely at the shading. How does the shading in the first shape change in the second shape?

The green shaded sections have become vertically striped.

The horizontally-striped sections have become clear.

> Now look at the first shape in the second pair. How will the shape change when these rules are applied?
>
> You know that the correct option must have a combination of clear sections and striped sections. You can therefore compare options A, B and D straight away.

© Brain Mapping Academy

Compare options A, B and D with the given shape. Which one has the shading in the correct position?

We know that:

 These horizontally striped sections must become clear

These green-shaded sections must become vertically striped

Hence option (A) must be the answer.

There are several variations of visual analogy questions that are based upon links with position. For some of these questions you will need to rely on your basic understanding of certain key maths topics, such as angles, symmetry, reflection and rotation.

Example 3

Which shape or pattern completes the second pair in the same way as the first pair?

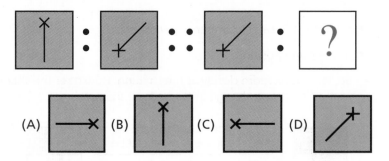

Answer: (A)

Explanation:

We can quickly note that in the first pair there is no change of shape and size but the figure is rotating anticlockwise through $135°(90° + 45°)$. The same relation is found in the answer figure (A).

REASONING TRAINER Plus

Example 4

Which shape or pattern completes the second pair in the same way as the first pair?

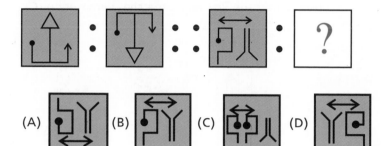

Answer: (A)

Explanation:

In the first pair, the second figure is the water image of the first figure. Similarly in the second pair, the required design will be the water image of the first figure.

Example 5

Which shape or pattern completes the second pair in the same way as the first pair?

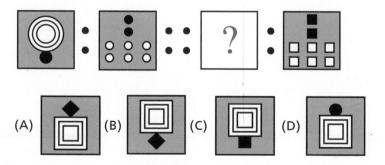

Answer: (C)

Explanation:

In the first pair, from figure (2) to (1), white circles are reduced to half the number and become concentric circles. Also the black circles are reduced to half their number and attached to the other circles. Similarly applying the rule for the second pair, we can observe that the first figure matches with option (C).

TRY THESE

1. Which shape of figure on the right completes the second pair in a similar way as in the first pair.

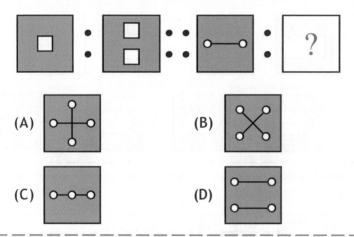

(A)

(B)

(C)

(D)

2. Which shape of figure on the right completes the second pair in a similar way as in the first pair.

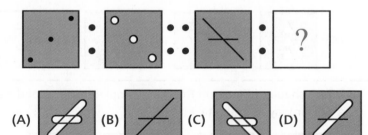

(A)   (B)   (C)   (D)

3. Which shape of figure on the right completes the second pair in a similar way as in the first pair.

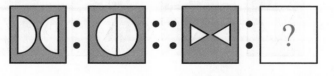

© Brain Mapping Academy

88

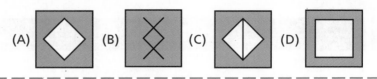

4. Which shape of figure on the right completes the second pair in a similar way as in the first pair.

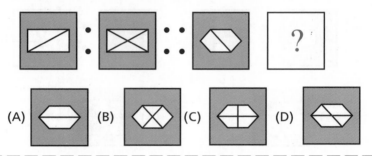

5. Which shape or pattern completes the second pair in the same way as the first pair?

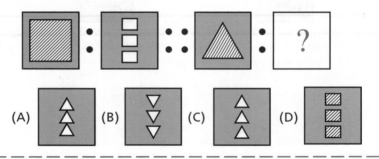

6. Which shape of figure on the right completes the second pair in a similar way as in the first pair.

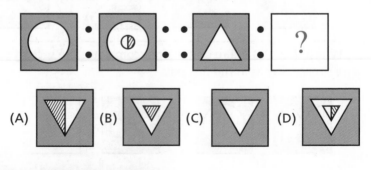

7.   Which shape of figure on the right completes the second pair in a similar way as in the first pair.

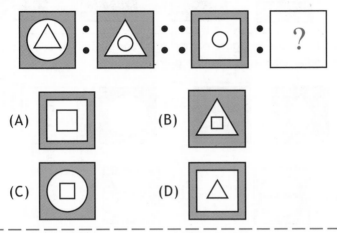

(A)   (B)

(C)   (D)

8.   Which shape of figure on the right completes the second pair in a similar way as in the first pair.

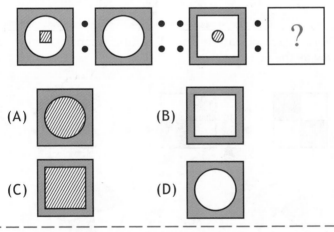

(A)   (B)

(C)   (D)

9.   Which shape or pattern completes the second pair in the same way as the first pair?

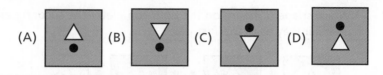

---

10. Which shape of figure on the right completes the second pair in a similar way as in the first pair.

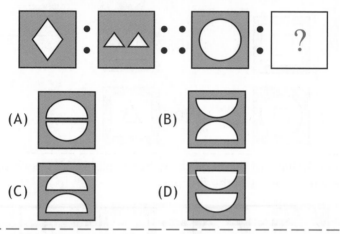

(A) (B)

(C) (D)

---

11. Which shape or pattern completes the second pair in the same way as the first pair?

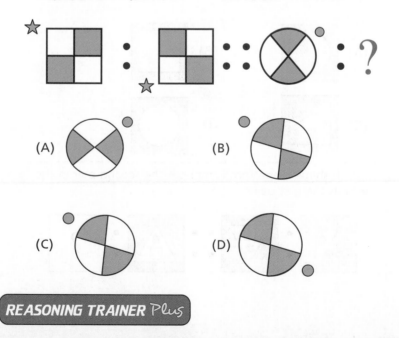

(A) (B)

(C) (D)

12. Which shape or pattern completes the second pair in the same way as the first pair?

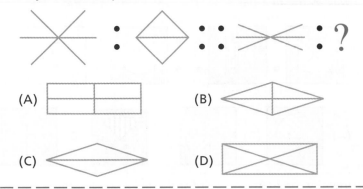

(A) [image]   (B) [image]

(C) [image]   (D) [image]

---

13. Which shape or pattern completes the second pair in the same way as the first pair?

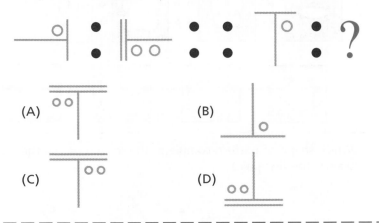

(A) [image]   (B) [image]

(C) [image]   (D) [image]

---

14. Identify the matching pair for the following figures.

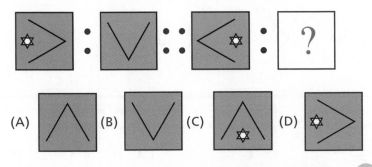

(A) [image] (B) [image] (C) [image] (D) [image]

15. Which shape or pattern completes the second pair in the same way as the first pair?

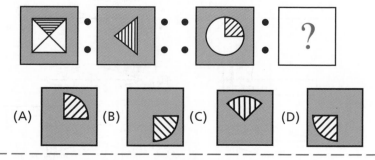

(A)　　(B)　　(C)　　(D)

16. Identify the matching pair for the following figures.

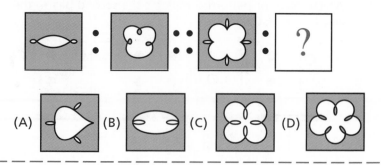

(A)　　(B)　　(C)　　(D)

17. Which shape or pattern completes the second pair in the same way as the first pair?

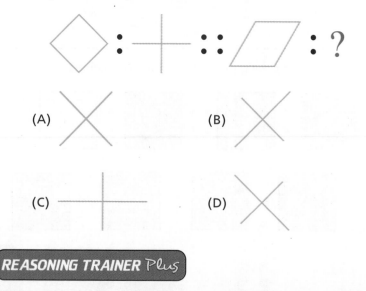

(A)　　(B)

(C)　　(D)

18. Which shape or pattern completes the second pair in the same way as the first pair?

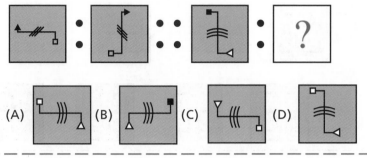

19. Identify the matching pair for the following figures.

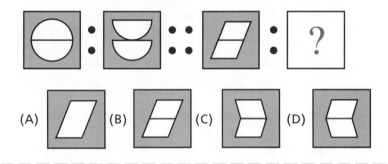

20. Which pattern completes the second pair in the same way as the first pair?

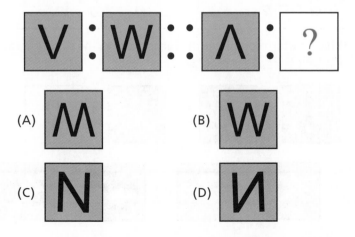

21. Which shape or pattern completes the second pair in the same way as the first pair?

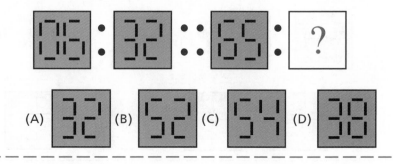

22. Identify the matching pair for the following figures.

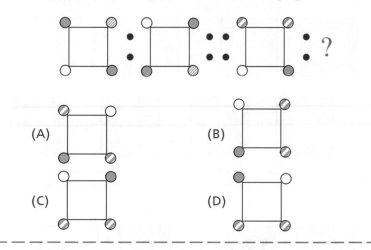

23. Which pattern completes the second pair in the same way as the first pair?

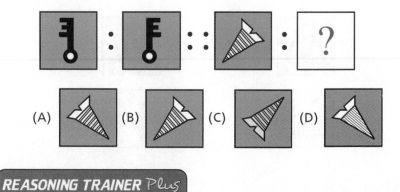

24. Which pattern completes the second pair in the same way as the first pair?

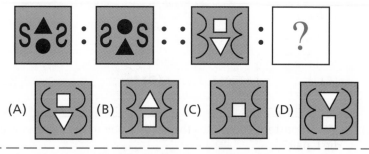

25. Identify the matching pair for the following figures.

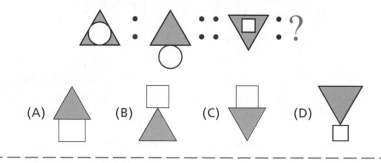

26. Which pattern completes the second pair in the same way as the first pair?

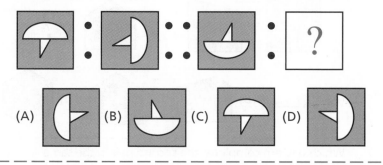

27. Identify the matching pair for the following figures.

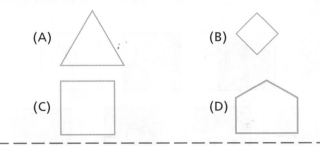

(A)　　　　　　(B)

(C)　　　　　　(D)

28. Which pattern completes the second pair in the same way as the first pair?

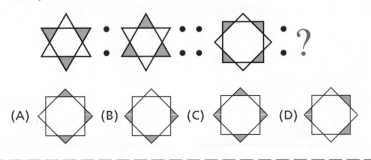

29. Which pattern completes the second pair in the same way as the first pair?

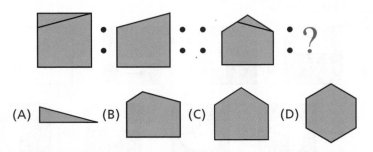

30. Which pattern completes the second pair in the same way as the first pair?

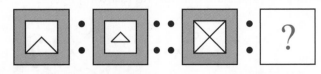

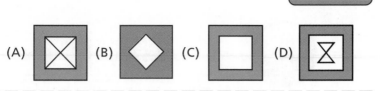

(A)   (B)   (C)   (D)

31. Which shape of figure on the right completes the second pair in a similar way as in the first pair.

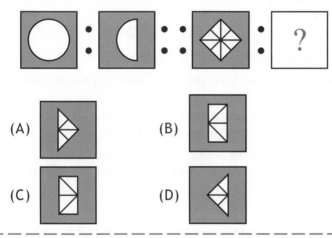

(A)   (B)

(C)   (D)

32. Which shape of figure on the right completes the second pair in a similar way as in the first pair.

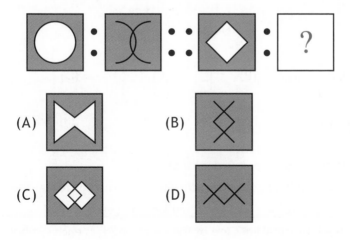

(A)   (B)

(C)   (D)

13 Chapter

Objective

- To identify and apply a rule.
- See shapes within shapes and patterns within patterns.
- Make reductions from the given set of objects or symbols.

The question types we will look at in this section are often referred to as sequence questions, you will need your observation and analytical skills to solve these question types.

Let's look at some examples, starting with one of the straight forward sequences you come across in various exams.

Example 1

1. What comes next?

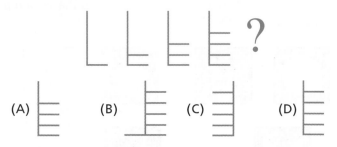

Answer: (D)

Explanation:

In this sequence, it is clear that

- Each symbol has one vertical line and some horizontal lines.
- The vertical line is of the same length in each symbol.
- The horizontal lines are of the same length in each symbol.
- All the horizontal lines point to the right.

REASONING TRAINER Plus

It seems easy to see then, that the only difference relates to the number of horizontal lines in each step of the sequence.

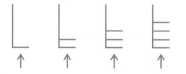

The number of horizontal lines increases by one in each step of the sequence.

1 lines 2 lines 3 lines 4 lines

Now compare the answer options with this rule and the common features listed above. Options (B) and (C) can be eliminated quickly, as they have horizontal lines pointing to the left.

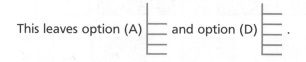

This leaves option (A) [image] and option (D) [image].

The last step in the given sequence has four horizontal lines. As the number of lines increases by one each time, the next step must have five lines. Option (D) is therefore the correct answer.

The next example is based on another element that you may find at the root of many sequence questions. It is often quite easy to see changes to this feature but be careful, it may not be the only rule that applies in a sequence!

Example 2

What comes next?

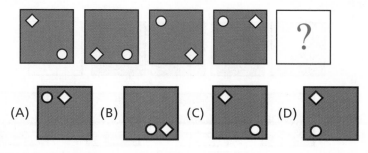

Answer: (C)

© Brain Mapping Academy

Explanation:

In each of the subsequent figures, '◇' shifts one adjacent vertex in anticlockwise direction and 'O' shifts to the opposite vertex after every two figures.

Hence, (C) is the next figure in the series.

Example 3

What comes next?

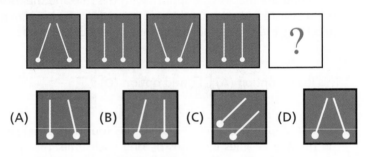

Answer: (D)

Explanation:

White circles at the end of the two lines move inside and then move apart in the pattern above.

Hence option (D) is the correct answer.

Example 4

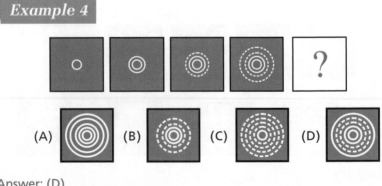

Answer: (D)

Explanation:

In each of the subsequent figures, one more circle forms after every two circles, the complete circle becomes dotted circles and vice versa.

TRY THESE

1. Find the figure which comes next in the series.

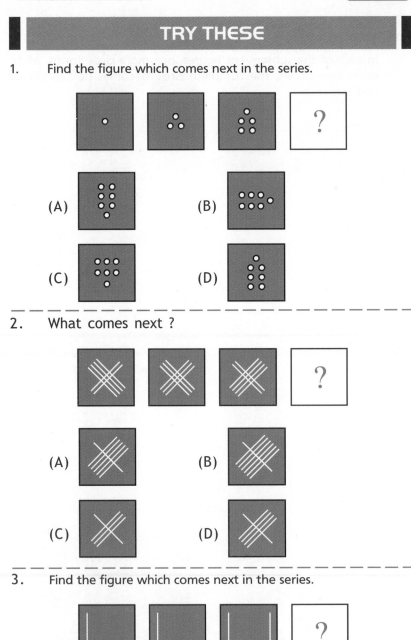

2. What comes next ?

3. Find the figure which comes next in the series.

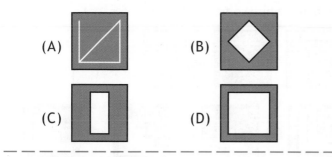

(A)   (B)

(C)   (D)

---

4.   What comes next ?

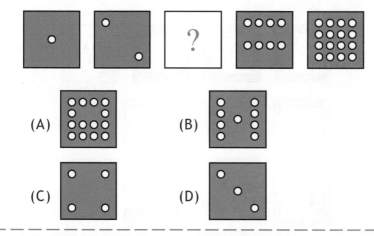

(A)   (B)

(C)   (D)

---

5.   Find the figure which comes next in the series.

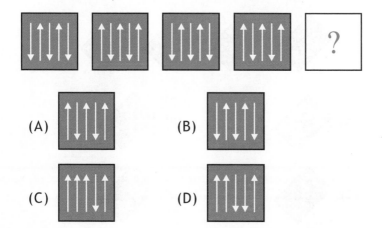

(A)   (B)

(C)   (D)

6. Find the figure which comes next in the series.

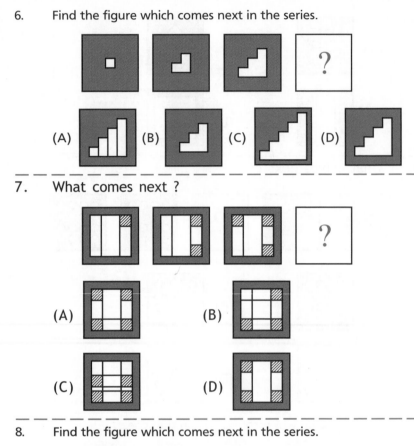

7. What comes next ?

8. Find the figure which comes next in the series.

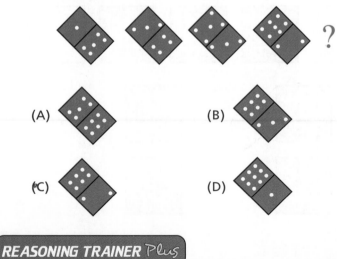

9. Find the figure which comes next in the series.

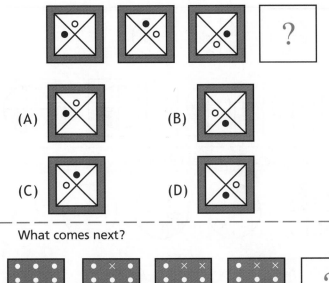

(A)   (B)

(C)   (D)

10. What comes next?

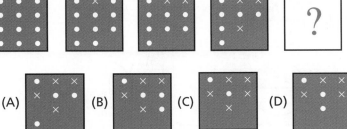

(A)   (B)   (C)   (D)

11. Find the figure which comes next in the series.

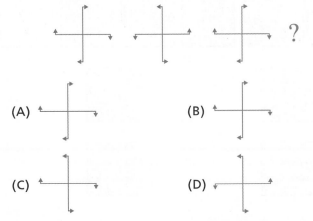

(A)   (B)

(C)   (D)

12. What comes next?

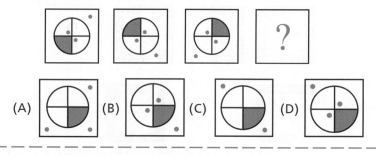

(A) (B) (C) (D)

13. Find the figure which comes next in the series.

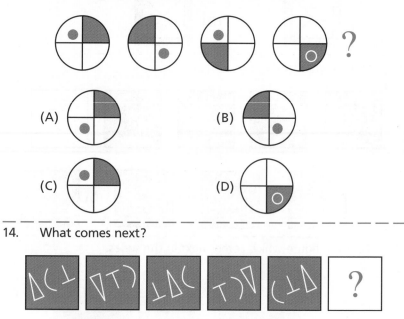

(A)   (B)

(C)   (D)

14. What comes next?

(A)   (B)

(C)   (D)

15. Find the figure which comes next in the series.

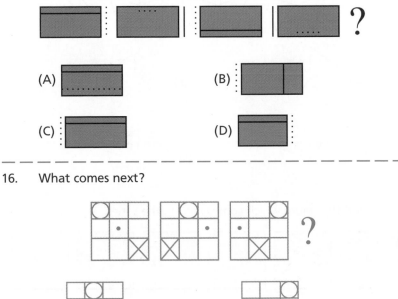

(A)   (B)

(C)   (D)

16. What comes next?

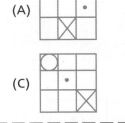   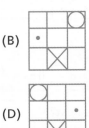

(A)   (B)

(C)   (D)

17. Find the figure which comes next in the series.

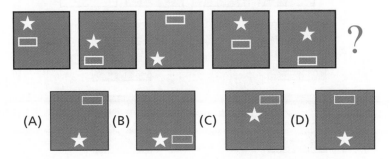

(A)   (B)   (C)   (D)

© Brain Mapping Academy

18. What comes next?

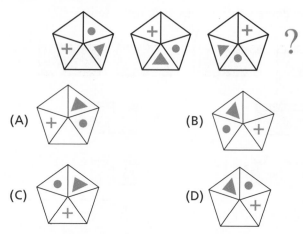

19. Find the figure which comes next in the series.

20. What comes next?

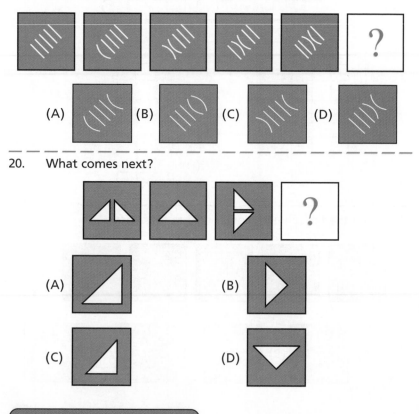

21. Find the figure which comes next in the series.

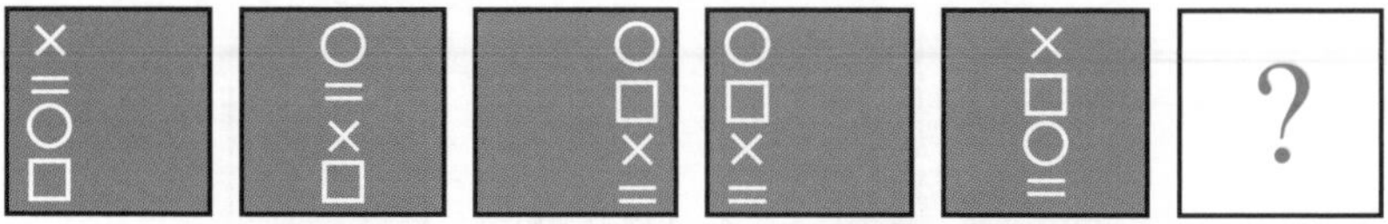

(A)

(B)

(C)

(D)

22. What comes next?

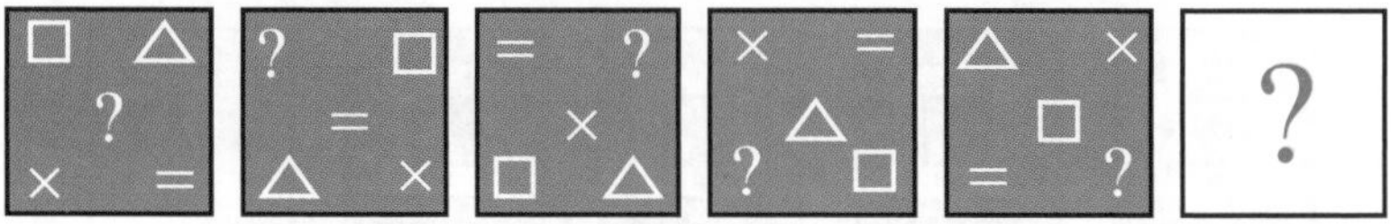

(A) 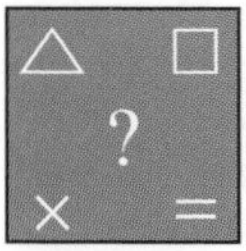 (B) 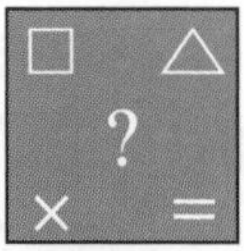 (C) 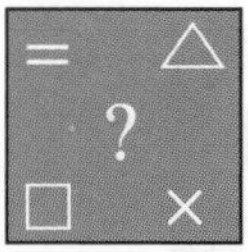 (D)

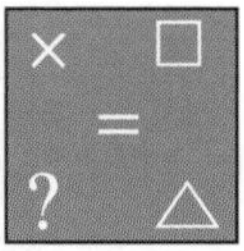

23. Find the figure which comes next in the series.

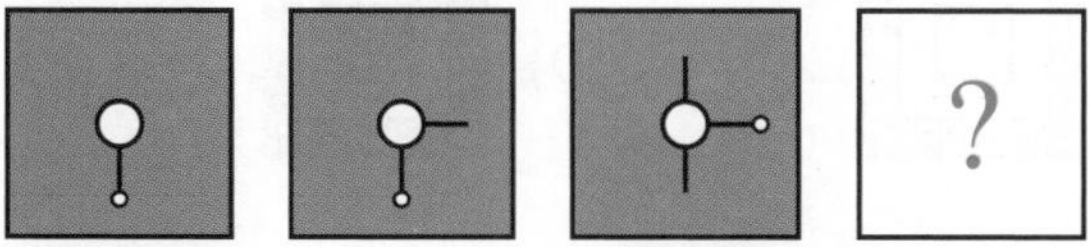

(A)

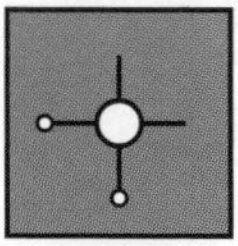

(B)

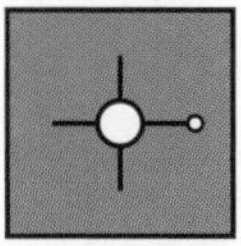

(C)

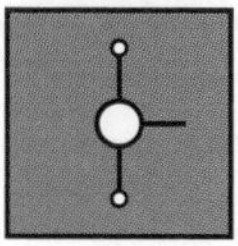

(D)

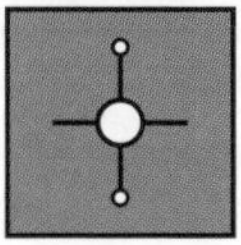

© Brain Mapping Academy

24. What comes next ?

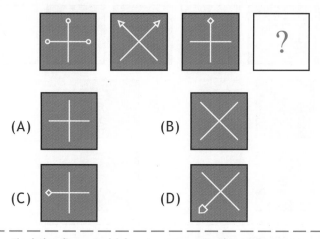

(A)   (B)

(C)   (D)

25. Find the figure which comes next in the series.

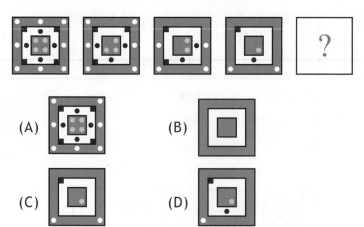

(A)   (B)

(C)   (D)

Objective ///

- To test if the reflection is the same as the original.

- To enhance your logical approach from different angles.

- To develop your visualisation power.

"The image of an object (either number or letter or figure) as seen in the mirror is called as Mirror Image. Mirror Image is also known as Reflection."

Mirror Images of numbers:

Numbers	Mirror Images	Numbers	Mirror Images
0	0	5	ꙅ
1	I	6	ɘ
2	ꙅ	7	⊤
3	Ɛ	8	8
4	↳	9	ǫ

Mirror images of capital letters:

Letter	Mirror Images	Letter	Mirror Images	Letter	Mirror Images	Letter	Mirror Images
A	A	G	Ə	N	И	U	U
B	ꓭ	H	H	O	O	V	V
C	Ɔ	I	I	P	ꟼ	W	W
D	ꓷ	J	Ⴑ	Q	Ọ	X	X
E	Ǝ	K	ꓘ	R	Я	Y	Y
F	ꟻ	L	⅃	S	Ꙅ	Z	Ƹ
		M	M	T	T		

© Brain Mapping Academy

Example 1

Choose the correct mirror image of the word "FUNDOO' from the options below.

(A) OOᗡИUᖴ (B) ᖴИUᗡOO (C) ᖴИUᗡOO (D) NUᖴᗡOO

Answer: (A)

Explanation:

 Step 1

To get the mirror image of FUNDOO arrange all the letters of the word in reverse order.

Reverse order = OODNUF

 Step 2

Take the mirror image of each letter separately.

$$F \longrightarrow ᖴ$$
$$U \longrightarrow U$$
$$N \longrightarrow И$$
$$D \longrightarrow ᗡ$$
$$O \longrightarrow O$$
$$O \longrightarrow O$$

Step 3

See the mirror image of 'FUNDOO'.

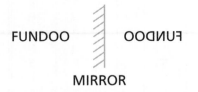

FUNDOO   OOᗡИUᖴ

MIRROR

So, option (A) is the answer.

Example 2

Choose the correct mirror image of the word 'DISCIPLINE' from the options below.

(A) ᗡIƧƆIꟼ⅃IИƎ (B) ᗡISCIP⅃IИƎ
(C) ƎИI⅃ꟼIƆƧIᗡ (D) ᗡIƧƆIꟼ⅃INE

Answer: (C)

Explanation:

Step 1

To get the mirror image of DISCIPLINE arrange all the letters of the word in reverse order.

Reverse order = ENILPICSID

Step 2

Take the mirror image of each word separately.

D → ᗡ
I → I
S → Ƨ
C → Ɔ
I → I
P → ꟼ
L → ⅃
I → I
N → И
E → Ǝ

Step 3

See the mirror image of 'DISCIPLINE'.

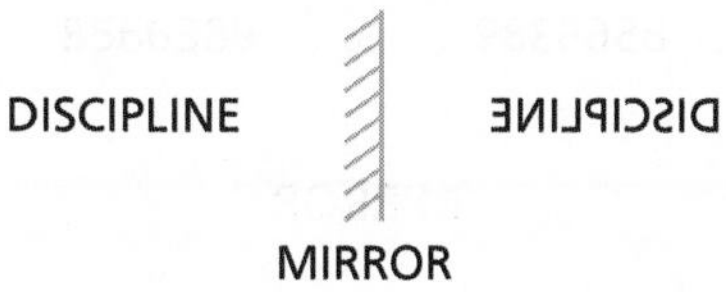

So, option (C) is the answer.

© Brain Mapping Academy

Example 3

Find the mirror image of '8566389'

(A) 9836658   (B) 8ᒲəəƐ8ℓ   (C) 8566Ɛ8ℓ   (D) ℓ8Ɛəəᒲ8

Answer: (D)

Explanation:

Step (1)

Arrange all the digits of a number '8566389' in the reverse order.

Reverse order = 9836658

Step (2)

Take the mirror image of each digit separately.

$$8 \longrightarrow 8$$
$$5 \longrightarrow ᒲ$$
$$6 \longrightarrow ə$$
$$6 \longrightarrow ə$$
$$3 \longrightarrow Ɛ$$
$$8 \longrightarrow 8$$
$$9 \longrightarrow ℓ$$

Step (3)

See the mirror image of the given number.

8566389 | ℓ8Ɛəəᒲ8

MIRROR

So, option (D) is answer.

REASONING TRAINER Plus

Example 4

By looking in a mirror, it appears that it is 6 : 30 in a clock. What is the real time?

(A) 6 : 30   (B) 5 : 30   (C) 6 : 00   (D) 4 : 30

Answer: (B)

Explanation:

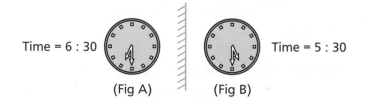

Time = 6 : 30   Time = 5 : 30

(Fig A)   (Fig B)

Clearly, fig (A) shows the time (6 : 30) in the clock as it appears in a mirror. Then its mirror – image i.e. fig (B) show the actual time in the clock i.e. 5 : 30.

Hint: You can solve such problems quickly if you remember sum of actual time and image time is always 12 hours.

Example 5

Identify the mirror image of the figure below.

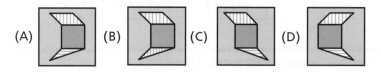

(A)   (B)   (C)   (D)

Answer: (A)

Explanation:

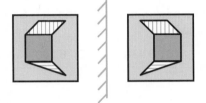

So, option (A) is answer.

Example 6

Identify the mirror image of the figure below.

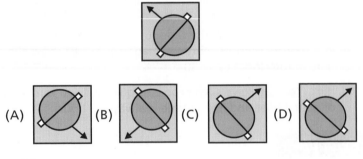

Answer: (C)

Explanation:

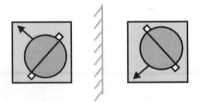

So, answer is the option (C).

TRY THESE

Directions for 1 to 3: **Find the mirror images of the words given below.**

1. PAINTED

   (A) ꓷƎTИIAꟼ   (B) ꓷƎTИIAꟼ

   (C) ꓷƎTИIAꟼ   (D) ꓷƎTИIAꟼ

2. NATIONAL

   (A) ꞀAИOITAИ   (B) ИAꞀIOИAꞀ

   (C) ꞀAИOIꞀAИ   (D) ꞀAИOITAИ

3. QUALITY

   (A) ꓘTIꞀAUꝹ   (B) YTIꞀAUꝹ

   (C) YTILAUꝹ   (D) YTILAUꝹ

- -

4. Identify the mirror image of the figure .

   (A) 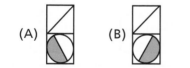 (B) (C) (D)

- -

5. Identify the mirror image of the figure .

   (A)   (B)   (C)   (D)

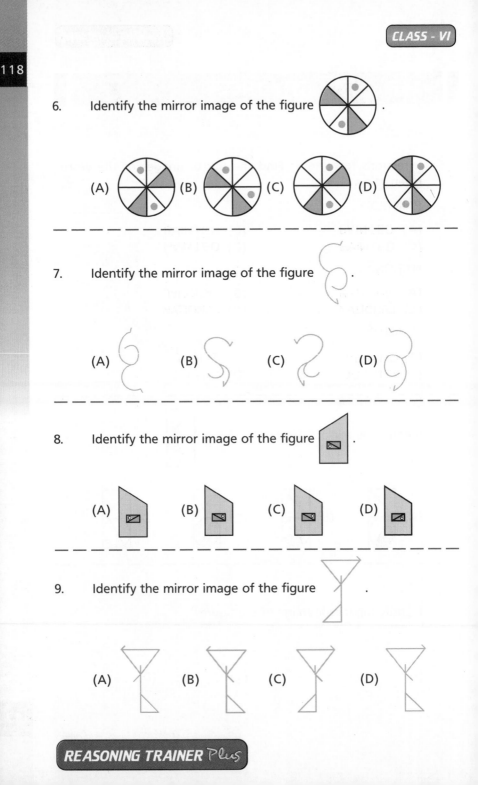

6. Identify the mirror image of the figure.

(A) (B) (C) (D)

7. Identify the mirror image of the figure.

(A) (B) (C) (D)

8. Identify the mirror image of the figure.

(A) (B) (C) (D)

9. Identify the mirror image of the figure.

(A) (B) (C) (D)

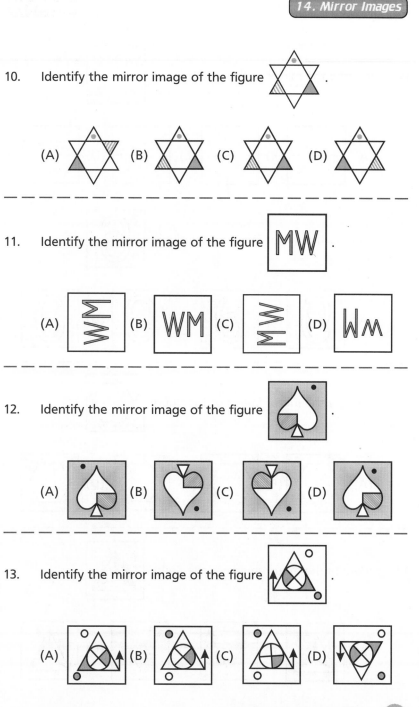

10. Identify the mirror image of the figure.

(A) (B) (C) (D)

11. Identify the mirror image of the figure MW.

(A) (B) WM (C) (D)

12. Identify the mirror image of the figure.

(A) (B) (C) (D)

13. Identify the mirror image of the figure.

(A) (B) (C) (D)

© Brain Mapping Academy

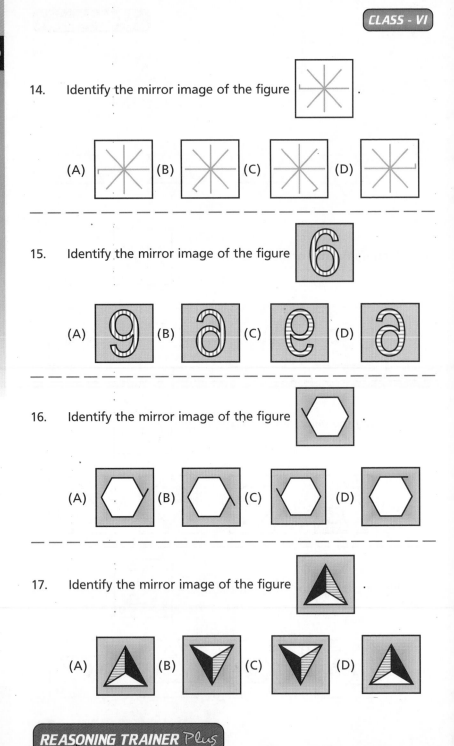

14. Identify the mirror image of the figure [ ].

(A) (B) (C) (D)

15. Identify the mirror image of the figure [ ].

(A) (B) (C) (D)

16. Identify the mirror image of the figure [ ].

(A) (B) (C) (D)

17. Identify the mirror image of the figure [ ].

(A) (B) (C) (D)

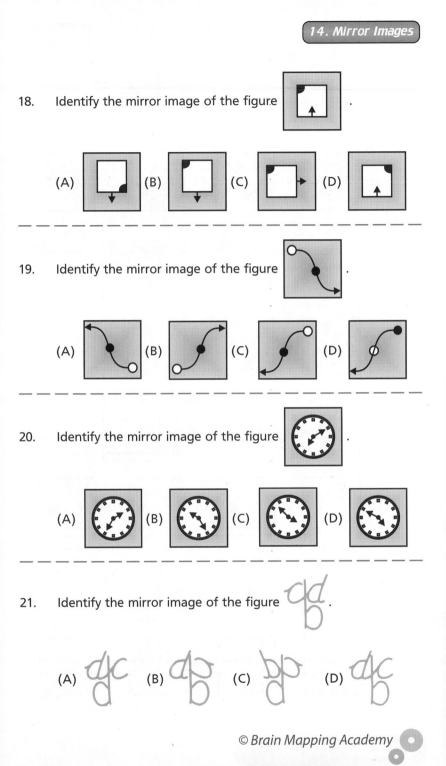

18. Identify the mirror image of the figure .

(A) (B) (C) (D)

19. Identify the mirror image of the figure .

(A) (B) (C) (D)

20. Identify the mirror image of the figure .

(A) (B) (C) (D)

21. Identify the mirror image of the figure .

(A) (B) (C) (D)

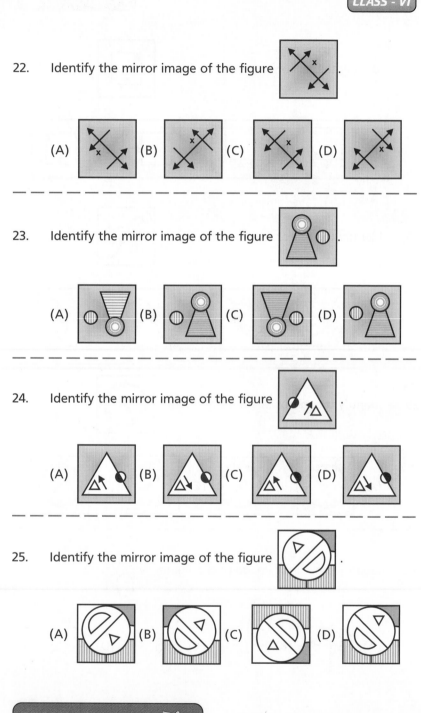

22. Identify the mirror image of the figure .

(A) (B) (C) (D)

23. Identify the mirror image of the figure .

(A) (B) (C) (D)

24. Identify the mirror image of the figure .

(A) (B) (C) (D)

25. Identify the mirror image of the figure .

(A) (B) (C) (D)

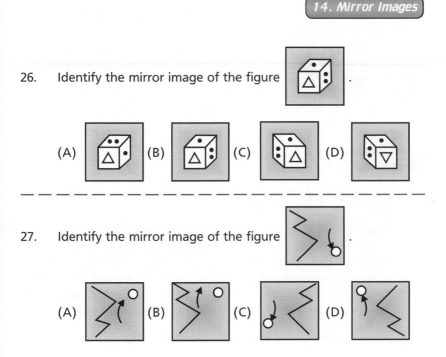

26. Identify the mirror image of the figure .

    (A)   (B)   (C)   (D)

27. Identify the mirror image of the figure .

    (A)   (B)   (C)   (D)

PAPER FOLDING

Objective

• Testing and visualization of spatial awareness and multidimentional shapes.

This type of questions are based on a transparent sheet. Some marks are made on the transparent sheet and a dotted line is made on the sheet. Then this sheet is folded along the dotted line. The candidate has to find out a figure among the answer figures, which resembles the pattern formed when the transparent sheet carrying a design is folded along the dotted line.

Steps to solve the problems on paper folding.

Step (1)

Decide the half plane which is dotted.

[See the empty half.]

Step (2)

Dotted part of the transparent sheet has been folded and placed over unfolded part.

[Imagine design of both parts in a half plane.]

Step (3)

See the combination of design at unfolded part.

[Imagine the design of both parts in a half plane]

[Note: The mirror image of the design on the right half of the sheet will reach to left half.]

Example 1

How does the shape [shape] look when folded along the dotted line?

(A) [figure] (B) [figure] (C) [figure] (D) [figure]

Answer: (A)

Explanation:

Step 1

Decide the half plane which is dotted.

[In the figure, upper half plane is dotted]

Step 2

Fold the paper

[While folding the paper. Upper circles will overlap the lower circles.]

Step 3

Seeing the lower half, the required answer is option (A).

Example 2

How does the shape look when folded along the dotted line?

© Brain Mapping Academy

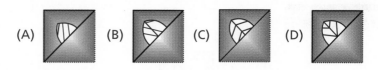

Answer: (D)

Explanation:

Step 1

Decide the half plane which is dotted. [Which is right half plane diagonally dotted.]

Step 2

Fold the right plane on unfolded one.

Step 3

Seeing the combined half plane, the appropriate answer is (D).

Example 3

How does the shape look when folded along the

dotted line??

Answer: (B)

Explanation:

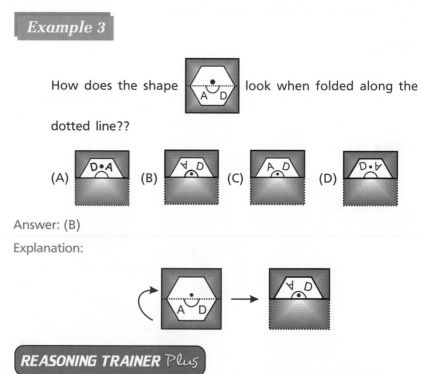

TRY THESE

1. How does the shape look when folded along the dotted line?

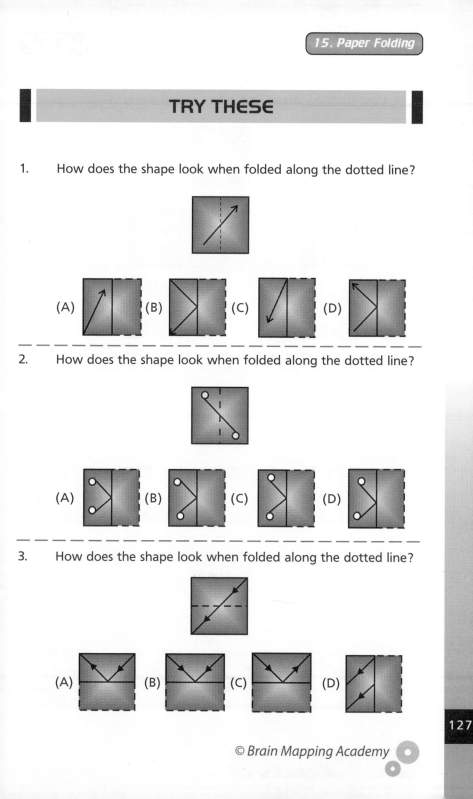

2. How does the shape look when folded along the dotted line?

3. How does the shape look when folded along the dotted line?

4. How does the shape look when folded along the dotted line?

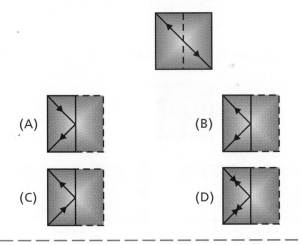

(A)   (B)

(C)   (D)

5. How does the shape look when folded along the dotted line?

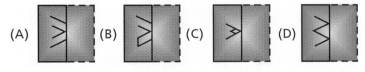

(A)   (B)   (C)   (D)

6. How does the shape look when folded along the dotted line?

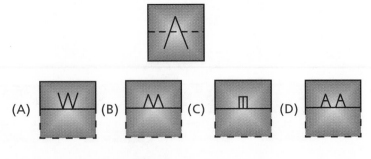

(A)   (B)   (C)   (D)

7. How does the shape look when folded along the dotted line?

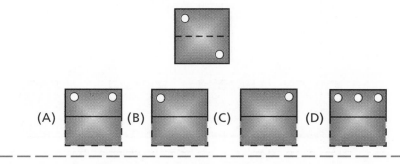

8. How does the shape look when folded along the dotted line?

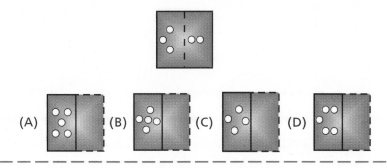

9. How does the shape look when folded along the dotted line?

(A)

(B)

(C)

(D)

10. How does the shape look when folded along the dotted line?

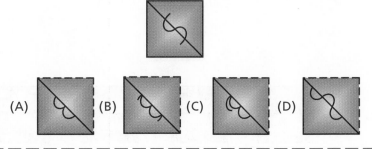

11. How does the shape look when folded along the dotted line?

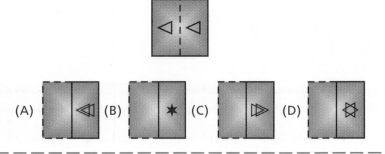

12. How does the shape look when folded along the dotted line?

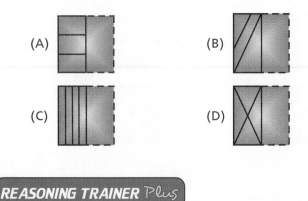

13. How does the shape look when folded along the dotted line?

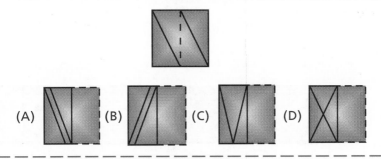

14. How does the shape look when folded along the dotted line?

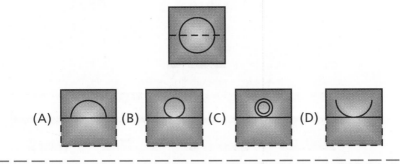

15. How does the shape look when folded along the dotted line?

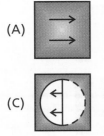 (A)   (B)

(C)   (D)

16. How does the shape look when folded along the dotted line?

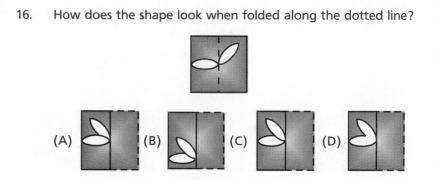

(A) (B) (C) (D)

17. How does the shape look when folded along the dotted line?

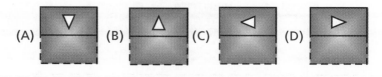

(A) (B) (C) (D)

18. How does the shape look when folded along the dotted line?

(A) (B)

(C) (D)

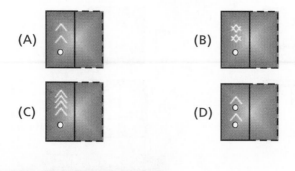

19. How does the shape look when folded along the dotted line?

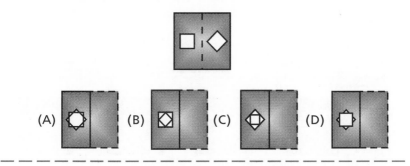

20. How does the shape look when folded along the dotted line?

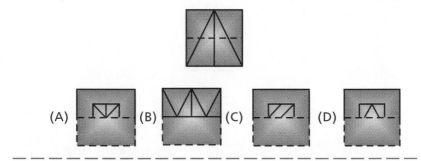

21. How does the shape look when folded along the dotted line?

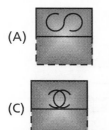

(A)   (B)

(C)   (D)

22. How does the shape look when folded along the dotted line?

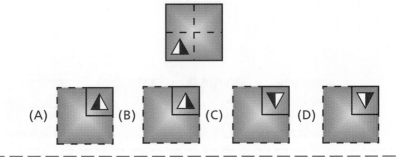

(A)   (B)   (C)   (D)

23. How does the shape look when folded along the dotted line?

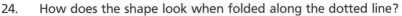

(A)   (B)   (C)   (D)

24. How does the shape look when folded along the dotted line?

(A)   (B)

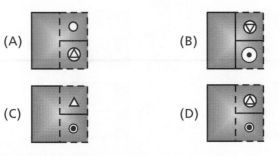

(C)   (D)

25. How does the shape look when folded along the dotted line?

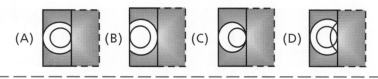

26. How does the shape look when folded along the dotted line?

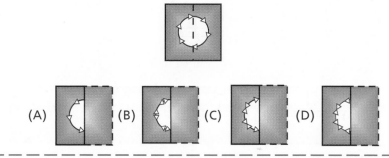

27. How does the shape look when folded along the dotted line?

(A)

(B)

(C)

(D)

28. How does the shape look when folded along the dotted line?

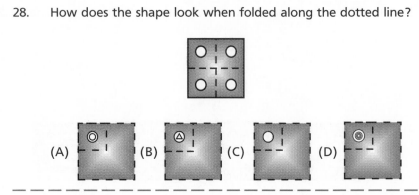

(A)   (B)   (C)   (D)

29. How does the shape look when folded along the dotted line?

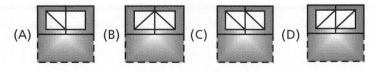

(A)   (B)   (C)   (D)

30. How does the shape look when folded along the dotted line?

(A)   (B)

(C)   (D)

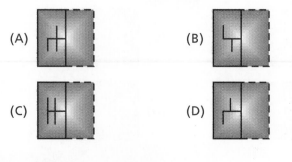

31. How does the shape look when folded along the dotted line?

(A) 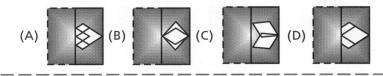 (B) (C) (D)

32. How does the shape look when folded along the dotted line?

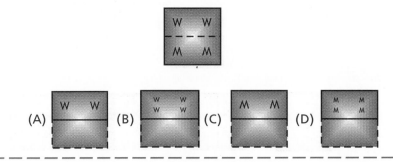

(A) (B) (C) (D)

33. How does the shape look when folded along the dotted line?

(A) 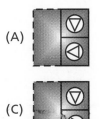 (B)

(C) (D)

137

34. How does the shape look when folded along the dotted line?

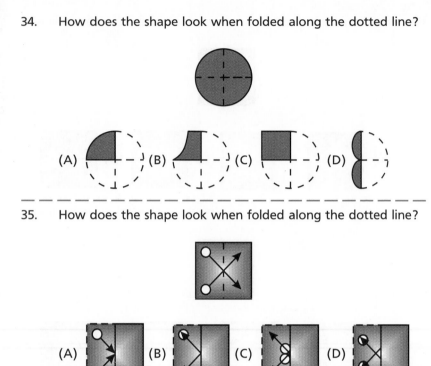

35. How does the shape look when folded along the dotted line?

Objective ///

- To inculcate the understanding of spatial awareness.

- Testing and visualization of spatial awareness and multidimentional shapes.

  The questions in this group are also called nets and they test your spatial awareness. Many people struggle with this type of questions as they have to think in three-dimensional terms. You need to be able to relate a two-dimensional outline, or net, to a three-dimensional shape and this can be hard to visualise.

  The following steps can help you to find the net for a given solid figure.

Step (1)

How do the faces or flaps of the shapes open out?

Step (2)

Count the number of faces or flaps.

Step (3)

Note also the shape and/or colour of each one.

Step (4)

Which answer is suitable?

© *Brain Mapping Academy*

Example 1

Which net makes the cube?

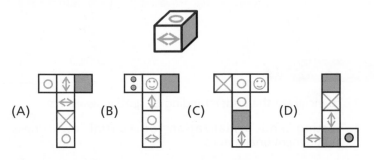

(A)   (B)   (C)   (D)

First, scan the nets and check whether any of the options can be eliminated straight away. As you can only see the top and two sides of the cube you do not know what symbols or shading will be on the rest of the faces. You can therefore only eliminate a net at this stage if it does not contain all three of the given cube faces.

Can any net be eliminated? Yes, option (D). It does not have a white circle so cannot be the answer.

This leaves options (A), (B) and (C) to consider in relation to the three rules.

It might be easier to look at option (C) first as this option only contains one double – ended arrow, whereas the other three options have two double – ended arrows.

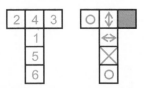

Concentrate on the faces that have the same symbols as shown in the cube. So for option (C) these are faces 4, 1, 5 and 6.

Faces 4 and 1 both show a circle. Think about which one of these could be showing on the top of the cube.

You know that face 1 and face 6 will be opposite to each other when the cube is folded. The cube shows the circle and the double

– ended arrow on adjacent faces, so face 1 cannot be the top of the cube.

Now look at the second circle. You know that face 4 and face 5 will be opposite each other when the cube is folded. The cube shows the circle and the shaded side on adjacent faces, so face 4 cannot be the top of the cube.

Option (C) can be discounted. Work through the remaining options from left to right and make sure you look at each one in the same way.

Here is option A.

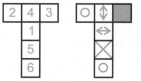

Faces 2 and 3 will be opposite when the net is folded but the cube shows the circle and black shaded side on adjacent faces. The circle on face 2 therefore cannot be on the top of the cube.

Now look at face 6. Faces 1 and 6 will also be opposite when the cube is formed. The double – ended arrow is shown on an adjacent face to the circle in the cube, so the arrow on face 1 cannot be the one shown.

This leaves faces 4, 3 and 6.

Which face borders will meet face 6 when the net is folded?

The borders of faces 4, 3 and 6 will meet to create two edges of the cube.

Option A could still be the answer. You will need to visualise these faces joining together to be sure.

Imagine folding the cube around face 1, making this the front of the cube.

Start by folding the dotted joint between face 4 and face 1 so face 4 forms the top of the cube.

Next, fold face 5 along the dotted joint so it forms the bottom of the cube.

Now fold face 6 so it forms a seam with face 4.

Look at the direction of the arrow in relation to the circle on face 6.

Is it the same orientation as in the given cube? No, here the double – ended arrow is pointing towards the circle. In the cube, the arrow is parallel to the circle. Option A can be eliminated.

Let's move on to option B.

Which, by this process of elimination, must be the answer. Remember though, even if you think you have found the correct answer, it is always best to double – check.

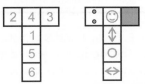

So, look at faces 3, 1, 5 and 6. How will the borders of these faces join to form edges of the cube? Follow the same step – by – step process as for the previous options.

Fold face 5 along the dotted joint, making it the top of the cube.

Then fold face 1 along the dotted joint to form the back of the cube.

Next, fold face 4 along the dotted joint, making this face the bottom of the cube.

Hence, answer must be (B).

REASONING TRAINER Plus

TRY THESE

1. How does the shape look when opened out?

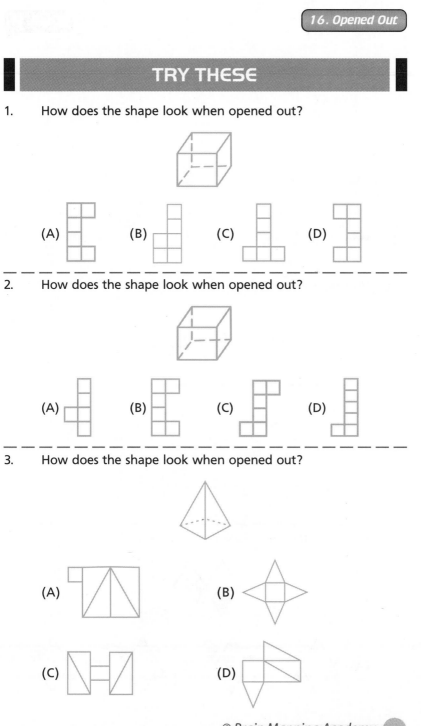

(A)　　(B)　　(C)　　(D)

2. How does the shape look when opened out?

(A)　　(B)　　(C)　　(D)

3. How does the shape look when opened out?

(A)　　(B)

(C)　　(D)

4. How does the shape look when opened out?

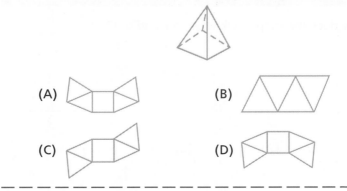

(A) (B)

(C) (D)

5. How does it look, when opened out?

(A) (B)

(C) (D)

6. How does the shape look when opened out?

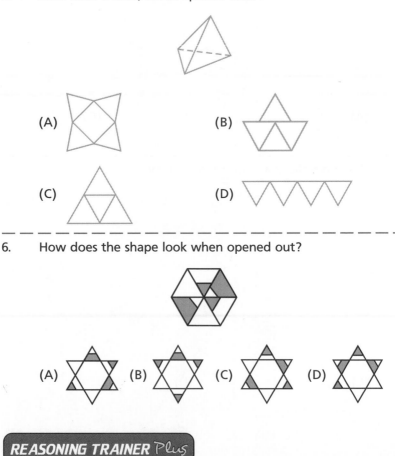

(A) (B) (C) (D)

7. How does the shape look when opened out?

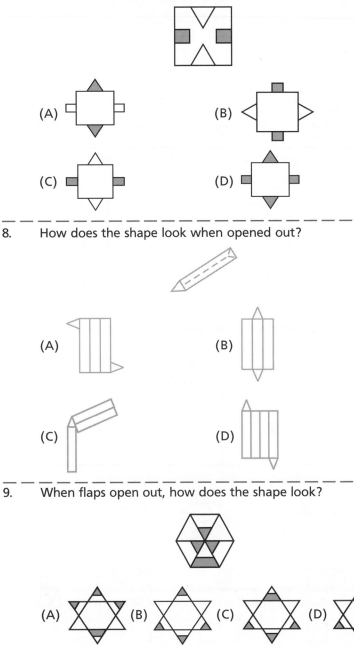

(A)

(B)

(C)

(D)

8. How does the shape look when opened out?

(A)

(B)

(C)

(D)

9. When flaps open out, how does the shape look?

(A) (B) (C) (D)

10. When flaps open out, how does the shape look?

(A)   (B)   (C)   (D)

11. When flaps open out, how does the shape look?

(A)   (B)   (C)   (D)

12. When flaps open out, how does the shape look?

(A)   (B)   (C)   (D)

13. When flaps open out, how does the shape look?

(A)   (B)   (C)   (D)

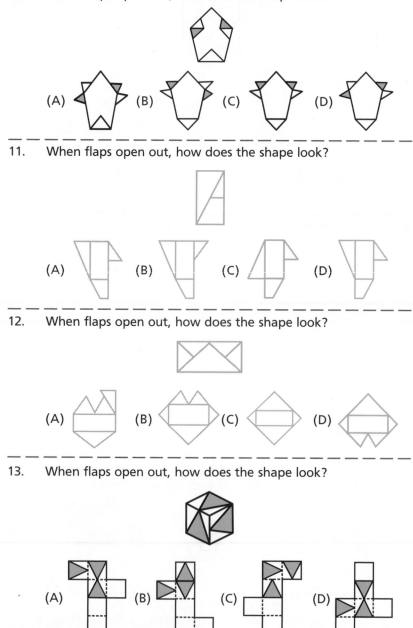

14. How does the shape look when opened out?

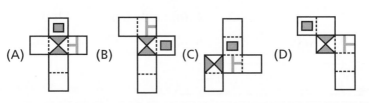

15. How does the shape look when opened out?

16. How does the shape look when opened out?

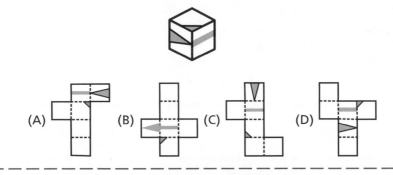

KEY

1 HIDDEN WORDS

1. (C)	3. (B)	5. (C)	7. (B)	9. (A)	11. (C)
2. (D)	4. (C)	6. (D)	8. (C)	10. (C)	12. (B)

2 JUMBLED WORDS

1. (C)	3. (B)	5. (C)	7. (B)	9. (D)	11. (C)
2. (B)	4. (A)	6. (A)	8. (C)	10. (B)	

3 ODD ONE OUT

1. (C)	4. (D)	7. (A)	10. (B)	13. (A)	16. (D)	19. (C)	22. (C)
2. (B)	5. (D)	8. (A)	11. (C)	14. (D)	17. (C)	20. (D)	23. (D)
3. (B)	6. (D)	9. (B)	12. (B)	15. (B)	18. (C)	21. (D)	24. (B)

4 MATCHING PAIRS

1. (D)	3. (A)	5. (B)	7. (B)	9. (A)
2. (B)	4. (B)	6. (A)	8. (D)	10. (C)

5 SERIES

1. (B)	6. (A)	11. (D)	16. (C)	21. (B)	26. (B)	31. (B)
2. (C)	7. (B)	12. (A)	17. (D)	22. (D)	27.(B)	32. (D)
3. (A)	8. (D)	13. (A)	18. (B)	23. (B)	28. (A)	33. (C)
4. (C)	9. (C)	14. (D)	19. (C)	24. (C)	29. (C)	34. (A)
5. (D)	10. (B)	15. (A)	20. (A)	25. (C)	30. (C)	

REASONING TRAINER *Plus*

6 USING LETTERS FOR NUMBERS

1. (D)	3. (A)	5. (B)	7. (B)	9. (A)	11. (A)	13. (A)	15. (C)
2. (B)	4. (C)	6. (D)	8. (C)	10. (C)	12. (C)	14. (C)	

7 PUZZLE TEST

1. (B)	4. (C)	7. (A)	10. (C)	13. (D)	16. (B)	19. (C)
2. (D)	5. (A)	8. (D)	11. (C)	14. (A)	17. (C)	20. (B)
3. (B)	6. (C)	9. (B)	12. (B)	15. (B)	18. (C)	

8 ANALYTICAL REASONING

1. (C)	4. (A)	7. (B)	10. (A)	13. (A)	16. (C)	19. (A)	22. (D)
2. (D)	5. (C)	8. (B)	11. (B)	14. (B)	17. (A)	20. (B)	
3. (C)	6. (C)	9. (C)	12. (D)	15. (B)	18. (C)	21. (C)	

9 MATHEMATICAL REASONING

1. (C)	5. (C)	9. (C)	13. (B)	17. (A)	21. (C)	25. (D)
2. (D)	6. (C)	10. (B)	14. (D)	18. (A)	22. (B)	
3. (A)	7. (B)	11. (C)	15. (C)	19. (B)	23. (C)	
4. (B)	8. (B)	12. (C)	16. (C)	20. (C)	24. (D)	

10 BREAK THE CODES

1. (D)	5. (D)	9. (A)	13. (C)	17. (D)	21. (C)	25. (A)	29. (D)
2. (B)	6. (D)	10. (A)	14. (B)	18. (B)	22. (B)	26. (C)	30. (C)
3. (B)	7. (A)	11. (C)	15. (B)	19. (A)	23. (A)	27. (B)	
4. (C)	8. (D)	12. (A)	16. (D)	20. (D)	24. (C)	28. (D)	

11   WHICH ONE IS DIFFERENT ?

1. (C)	5. (A)	9. (C)	13. (A)	17. (A)	21. (C)	25. (A)	29. (A)
2. (B)	6. (D)	10. (C)	14. (D)	18. (D)	22. (B)	26. (B)	30. (C)
3. (C)	7. (B)	11. (B)	15. (B)	19. (A)	23. (D)	27. (C)	
4. (B)	8. (A)	12. (C)	16. (D)	20. (B)	24. (C)	28. (D)	

12   ANALOGY

1. (D)	5. (C)	9. (D)	13. (D)	17. (B)	21. (A)	25. (D)	29. (B)
2. (A)	6. (D)	10. (C)	14. (A)	18. (B)	22. (B)	26. (A)	30. (D)
3. (C)	7. (C)	11. (C)	15. (B)	19. (C)	23. (A)	27. (B)	31. (D)
4. (B)	8. (B)	12. (C)	16. (D)	20. (A)	24. (D)	28. (C)	32. (B)

13   WHAT COMES NEXT ?

1. (D)	5. (B)	9. (B)	13. (C)	17. (A)	21. (C)	25. (B)
2. (A)	6. (D)	10. (C)	14. (D)	18. (B)	22. (B)	
3. (D)	7. (D)	11. (D)	15. (D)	19. (D)	23. (B)	
4. (C)	8. (D)	12. (D)	16. (C)	20. (B)	24. (B)	

14   MIRROR IMAGES

1. (B)	6. (A)	11. (B)	16. (A)	21. (C)	26. (C)
2. (A)	7. (B)	12. (A)	17. (A)	22. (B)	27. (C)
3. (B)	8. (D)	13. (A)	18. (D)	23. (B)	
4. (A)	9. (B)	14. (D)	19. (C)	24. (A)	
5. (D)	10. (D)	15. (B)	20. (D)	25. (B)	

REASONING TRAINER Plus

15   PAPER FOLDING

1. (D)	7. (A)	13. (D)	19. (A)	25. (D)	31. (A)
2. (C)	8. (B)	14. (A)	20. (B)	26. (B)	32. (A)
3. (A)	9. (B)	15. (C)	21. (D)	27. (C)	33. (C)
4. (B)	10. (B)	16. (C)	22. (C)	28. (C)	34. (A)
5. (D)	11. (D)	17. (B)	23. (C)	29. (D)	35. (B)
6. (A)	12. (D)	18. (A)	24. (B)	30. (C)	

16   OPENED OUT

1. (C)	3. (B)	5. (C)	7. (C)	9. (D)	11. (A)	13. (A)	15. (A)
2. (C)	4. (C)	6. (C)	8. (B)	10. (D)	12. (B)	14. (B)	16. (B)